To Fra

Osiris

To my parents

BOJANA MOJSOV

OSIRIS

Death and Afterlife
of a God

Blackwell
Publishing

BLACKWELL PUBLISHING

350 Main Street, Malden, MA 02148-5020, USA
9600 Garsington Road, Oxford OX4 2DQ, UK
550 Swanston Street, Carlton, Victoria 3053, Australia

The right of Bojana Mojsov to be identified as the Author of this Work has been
asserted in accordance with the UK Copyright, Designs, and Patents Act 1988.

First published 2005 by Blackwell Publishing Ltd

1   2005

Library of Congress Cataloging-in-Publication Data

Mojsov, Bojana.
    Osiris: death and afterlife of a god/Bojana Mojsov.
        p. cm.
    Includes bibliographical references.
        ISBN-13: 978-1-4051-1073-0 (hard cover: alk. paper)
        ISBN-13: 978-1-4051-3179-7 (pbk.: alk. paper)
        ISBN-10: 1-4051-1073-2 (hard cover: alk. paper)
        ISBN-10: 1-4051-3179-9 (pbk.: alk. paper)
    1. Osiris (Egyptian deity)—Cult–History.   2. Mysteries, Religious—History.
3. Christianity—Origin. I. Title.

    BL2450.07M65 2005
    299'.312113—dc22   2004028424

A catalogue record for this title is available from the British Library.

Set in 10/13pt Photina
by Graphicraft Limited, Hong Kong
Printed and bound in the United Kingdom
by TJ International Ltd, Padstow, Cornwall

The publisher's policy is to use permanent paper from mills that operate
a sustainable forestry policy, and which has been manufactured from
pulp processed using acid-free and elementary chlorine-free practices.
Furthermore, the publisher ensures that the text paper and cover board
used have met acceptable environmental accreditation standards.

For further information on Blackwell Publishing, visit our website:
www.blackwellpublishing.com

CONTENTS

PLATES

FIGURES

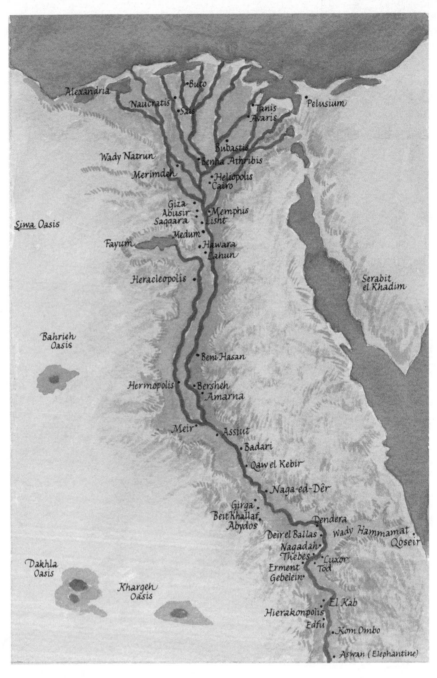

1 Map of Egypt

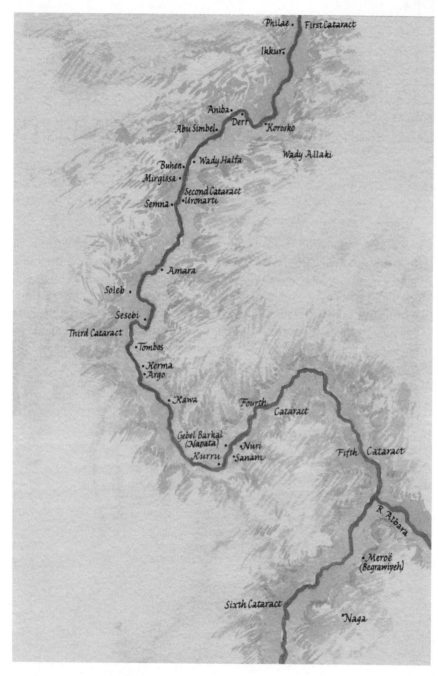

2 Map of Sudan (Zoran Grebenarevic)

ACKNOWLEDGMENTS

I would like to thank all those who helped with their advice and scrutiny in writing and producing this book. Among them, Shane Abdelnour, Al Bertrand, Roland Chambers, Matthew Connolly, Layla Doss, Roger Munro, Raymond Stock, and Patrick Werr. Julian Reilly patiently put up with the various stages of writing at the kitchen table, which at times was not unlike rowing the boat of Millions of Years through the perilous regions of the netherworld. Zoran Grebenarevic generously supplied the maps of Egypt and Sudan, as well as highly spirited comments about the text. Stevan Marinkovic and Nenad Mikalacki – Django – provided incomparable assistance with the color plates and the front-page design and Fabrice Leroux with the line drawings. All of them made their contributions to putting *Osiris* together and have breathed their spirits into the book.

INTRODUCTION

Osiris resplendent, with his tall, plumed crown, sits enthroned at the gate of the netherworld, surrounded by the court of immortals. Jackal-headed Anubis leads the deceased to him; hawk-headed Horus stands in attendance of the final verdict on the soul's justification; ibis-headed Thoth grasps the pen and tablet to record the judgment. Osiris, pointing his scepter of eternal kingship, the shepherd's crook, addresses the approaching soul: "Enter, because you know."

The myth of Osiris, judge of souls in the netherworld and shepherd to immortality, was at the heart of ancient Egypt. Yet, because of the peculiar nature of their religion, the Egyptians never took the trouble to write down or explain his myth. It was up to the Greek philosopher Plutarch, who visited Egypt in the first century AD, to record the first continuous account of the myth of Osiris. In Egypt, the death and resurrection of Osiris were matters not to be divulged – a Great Mystery.

Egyptian history lasted for more than three thousand years, longer than our own. It was recorded in full scope by the Egyptian priest Manetho in the third century BC at the request of Ptolemy I, then Greek ruler of Egypt. Manetho divided the kings and queens of Egypt into 30 ruling families or dynasties, a simple and durable convention still followed by modern scholars. Manetho's original book, called *Aegyptiaca*, no longer exists (it may have perished when the library of Alexandria was burned), but we have partial copies of it by Josephus, Africanus, Eusebius, and Syncellus.

The terms Old, Middle, and New Kingdom are modern designations used for convenience. So are the three Intermediate Periods. They break down the long history of Egypt into three stable categories interrupted by three divisions. After the end of the Third Intermediate Period, we have 600 years more Egyptian history, usually described as the Late Period. During the Late Period, Egypt was ruled by the last three native Egyptian dynasties before being conquered by foreigners – Persians, Greeks, and Romans.

The present book begins with the myth of Osiris. The story mainly relies on Plutarch's account, though I have abbreviated it, leaving out the Greek names of the gods and the complex genealogies that relate the Greek gods to the Egyptian. In the following chapters, I trace the story of Osiris to prehistoric Egypt and its appearance among the sacred kings of the Nile valley. For millennia, the flood of the Nile had been of central importance to life in the valley – this area has some of the lowest rainfall in the world and people had always depended on the river to water their fields. The sacrifice of the king, Son of the Nile and Father of the Tribe, was linked with the life of the river. Osiris was buried when the flood abated, before the season of plowing. At harvest time at the spring equinox, his loving wife Isis breathed life into his body and he engendered a son. Theirs was the Savior Child of light, born at the winter solstice with the sun. From time immemorial the myth of Osiris had explained the unfathomable cycles of nature.

As Egyptian history unfolded, the cult of Osiris grew in popularity. In the Middle Kingdom (2055–1650 BC) he assumed the role of the Great Judge of souls in the netherworld who dispensed bread and beer to the justified souls. Every year in the town of Abydos his death and resurrection after three days were celebrated in a publicly enacted passion play called the Mysteries of Osiris. In the New Kingdom (1550–1069 BC), after the rise of the sun cult and the monotheistic religion introduced by King Akhenaton, the cult of Osiris clasped hands with the cult of Ra and Osiris became an enlightened savior-god, shepherd to immortality for ordinary people. By the Late Period (1069–332 BC), his cult had spread around the Mediterranean. As the redemptive figure of the Egyptian god loomed large over the ancient world, Isis came to be worshipped as the Primordial Virgin and their child as the Savior of the World.

When the Greeks established themselves as rulers in Alexandria (332–30 BC), they continued to worship Osiris as Sarapis and passed his cult on to the Romans. Through the Greeks the Hellenized version of the Osiris myth endured in Western culture. The rise of science and philosophy in Alexandria paved the way for the rich spiritual legacy of late antiquity. It was in Roman Alexandria (30 BC – AD 394) that the new Christian religion blossomed, inspired by the writings of the Egyptian, Greek, and Jewish philosophers. By then Osiris had become, in the words of Carl Jung, "the Patriarch of all the Near Eastern savior-figures."

A list of Egyptian gods and goddesses is given at the beginning of this book for quick reference, while a more detailed glossary is provided at the end. A chronological table for three and a half thousand years of Egyptian history through which the myth evolved is also at the end of the book (it follows the dates in the *Oxford History of Egypt*, cited in the bibliography). I should point out that in my abbreviated version of Egyptian history I have set together the

Third Intermediate Period and the Late Period in one chapter. In the text, I have sometimes used the Egyptian way of counting the years of rule: the accession of every king was marked as year one of king NN and years of rule were then added from year one on. Thus, for example, year seventeen of Akhenaton denotes the seventeenth year after he came to the throne.

A brief note about the use of Egyptian words: I have used the word "pharaoh" to describe the first kings of Egypt, even though the earliest mention of this word in Egyptian records dates to the New Kingdom and the archives of Akhenaton. Literally, the biblical word "pharaoh" – the Egyptian "per a'at" – meant "great house." This phrase was used in the same way as the phrases the Great Porte and the White House are used to designate the Turkish sultan and president of the United States. I have taken the liberty of calling the first kings of Egypt pharaohs because of the absolutist meaning the word implies.

In the writing of the names of the goddesses Nout and Mout as well as in related names, such as Senmout, I have chosen the spelling that implies the long "u" in pronouncing them. In the spelling of the names of kings I have generally followed the Egyptian pronunciation. At times, however, such as with the names of kings Apries, Amasis, and Nectanebo, I used the Greek ones, because of their more common use. In the chronology at the end of the book, where space permitted, I have given both versions side by side. In the names of towns I have also used Greek names followed by the modern names in brackets, omitting the ancient Egyptian names in order to avoid clutter.

Many sources quoted in the present book come from the writings of Herodotus, Diodorus, and Plutarch. Though these Greek writers visited Egypt rather late in her history, their descriptions of Egyptian customs still convey the immediacy of eyewitness accounts. I have briefly described their lives and work, as well as those of other ancient writers mentioned in the book, in the glossary.

The terms "Upper Egypt" and "Lower Egypt," contrary to expectation, refer respectively to the south and north. Because the Nile flows from south to north, the Upper Nile is in the south and the Lower Nile is in the north.

A final note: in the old days the flooding of the Nile was the main event of the Egyptian year. This came to an end with the completion of the Assuan High Dam in 1965. From then on, the Nile no longer floods in Egypt. The country has become industrialized and Egyptian culture has changed – the oneness of the people and the soil, the role of the river as the harbinger of life, the perception of the cycle of the seasons and of time. I have looked below the High Dam to Sudan to resuscitate the past and experience the power of the Nile inundation. It is there than one can still see the full impact of the flood and its effect on the life of the people, particularly on the southern tribes who still practice their age-old customs.

EGYPTIAN GODS AND GODDESSES

Amun
(Amon, Amen) "the hidden one." Theban god of the air and of the breath of life; the ram was sacred to him.

Andjety
"he who came from the Anedj waters"; the original god of Djedu-Busiris who became assimilated with Osiris.

Anubis
the jackal-headed god of embalming, said to have helped Isis find and preserve the body of Osiris. Anubis was the counter of hearts who greeted the dead on their entry to the netherworld; he connected the visible and the invisible worlds.

Apep
(Apophis) the serpent of darkness and oblivion, the nemesis of Ra.

Apis
the bull of Memphis, the living incarnation of Ptah. The king's power animal, associated with Osiris in the netherworld. At the burial of a king a bull was sacrificed and buried with him to assist on the journey to the hereafter.

Aton
the sun disk, a manifestation of the sun god championed by Akhenaton.

Atum
(Tem, Temu, Atem) "the undifferentiated one," the primal element, the creator dwelling in the primeval waters as a spirit. One of the solar trinity worshiped at Heliopolis, he brought himself into being by uttering his own name and then created the universe. The shrew, mouse, and ichneumon were sacred to him. His name may be at the root of the biblical "Adam" and the Greek "atom."

Bastet the goddess of Bubastis, patron of pleasure and protector from evil spirits. The cat was sacred to her.

Bennu the mythical phoenix, worshiped at Heliopolis as the soul of Osiris and symbol of Ra's renewal. His name meant "to rise, shine." His appearance was that of a heron with long plumes falling from the back of his head.

Bes leonine dwarf-god, whose grotesque appearance was intended to frighten away evil spirits. He safeguarded new mothers and newborn children and was in charge of music, dance, and jollity. Popular among kings and commoners, he was worshiped as the protector of domestic happiness and even supervisor of the bed and its pleasures.

Geb son of Shu (air) and Tefnut (moisture), god of the earth. Represented as a man with a goose on his head. It is peculiar to Egypt that the earth was always envisioned as a male; grammatically as a noun it had the male gender. In the Book of the Dead, Geb was called "the great cackler."

Hapi personification of the Nile, represented as a portly figure bearing food offerings.

Harpocrates Greek for the Egyptian "Hor-pa-khered," Horus the Child.

Hathor "the house of Horus," the primeval goddess represented as a cow, renowned as the Great Mother, goddess of love, beauty, and music. Her instrument was the sistrum, a musical rattle of metal and wood. It was used on festive occasions and to frighten demons. Her cult center was at Dendera. From the Late Period on, she was celebrated in the sacred marriage.

Heqat the frog, related to fertility. She presided over births as a midwife.

Hor-sa-Iset Horus-the-son-of-Isis.

Horus "the distant one," the falcon god of the sky, protector of kingship. His early cult center was at Hieraconpolis, the later ones at Edfu and Kom Ombo.

Ihy the golden calf, the child of Hathor.

Isis one of the four children of Geb (earth) and Nout (sky), sister and wife of Osiris, mother of Horus-the-child. The star Sirius (the Egyptian Sepdet) was associated with her. Her titles included those of Mother of God, Great of Magic, Mistress of Heaven and the New Year, Star of the Sea (in Alexandria), Virgin of the World (in the Hermetic tradition).

Khenti Amentiu   "foremost of the Land of the West," the jackal-god of Abydos who was assimilated with Osiris.

Khepri   the scarab beetle, the rising sun, part of the solar trinity of Heliopolis as Khepri-Ra-Atum.

Khnum   "the molder," the divine potter who fashioned the bodies of people from clay. The ram-headed god of Elephantine island at Assuan, protector of the Nile.

Khonsu   "one who travels across the sky," the moon god, child of Amun and Mout, worshiped at Thebes. His statues were believed to have the power of casting out demons.

Ma'at   goddess of justice and truth. The measuring scales were her attribute.

Meretseger   "she who loves silence," the goddess of the Theban necropolis.

Min   god of creative energy who gave all living things the power to reproduce themselves, represented as an ithyphallic figure and worshiped as a fertility god. The lettuce plant, believed to possess aphrodisiac powers, was sacred to him. His cult center was at Koptos.

Mout   wife of Amun, mother of Khonsu.

Nefertem   the lotus child, son of Ptah and Sakhmet.

Neith   war goddess of Sais who taught mortals the art of weaving. The bow and two crossed arrows were her symbols.

Nekhbet   the vulture, ancient protector-goddess of Upper Egypt.

Nephthys   (Egyptian Neb-hat) "mistress of the house," one of the daughters of Geb and Nout, sister of Osiris and Isis, wife of Seth.

Noun   "father of the gods," the primeval ocean out of whom all life emerged.

Nout   "mother of the gods," goddess of the sky, daughter of Shu and Tefnet, worshiped as the Great Mother, whose body encompassed the sun, moon, and all the stars.

Osiris   the son of Geb and Nout. Primeval king of Egypt who brought civilization to his people. Related with the constellation of Orion (the Egyptian Sah). God

	of the resurrection who presided over the judgment of the soul.
Ptah	god of Memphis, maker of all visible forms and patron of art and artisans, represented in human form wearing the skull-cap of workmen. Worshiped as a primeval creator god, whose word inspired Atum's creation.
Ra	the primeval sun-god of Heliopolis. The visible body of the sun, worshiped as the trinity of Khepri-Ra-Atum.
Sakhmet	"the powerful one," lion-headed goddess whose statues were believed to cure illnesses. Consort of Ptah, mother of Nefertem.
Sarapis	Osiris-Apis, a composite god promoted by the Ptolemies.
Selket	the scorpion-goddess, protector of coffins and funerary equipment. She was associated with the scorching heat of the Egyptian desert; a stellar constellation was sacred to her.
Seth	the adversary, son of Geb and Nout, brother of Osiris, god of the desert and the oases. His symbol was a mythical desert hound, but he was also associated with the serpent, ass, pig, hippopotamus, crocodile, and fish. His domain was the red desert and he was a red god. Only red oxen were sacrificed to him. Red-haired men were believed to be his representatives on earth. His name may be at the root of the Hebrew word "sheitan" (the Christian "satan") that originally meant "adversary."
Seven Hathors	goddesses of destiny who prophesized at birth the events to come in the life of the newborn child. In the mamisi-birth houses of Greco-Roman Egypt they were shown assisting at royal births.
Shu	"the uplifter," god of the air, father of Geb and Nout.
Sobek	the crocodile god. His cult centers were in the Fayoum oasis and at Kom Ombo, where he was worshiped jointly with Horus.
Sokar	mummified falcon who watched over cemeteries. His name is contained in that of Saqqara, the earliest necropolis of Memphis.
Taweret	"the great earth (mother)," a pregnant hippopotamus who protected women in pregnancy and childbirth. A stellar constellation was sacred to her.

Tefnet goddess of moisture, mother of Geb and Nout.

Thoth god of magic, divine intelligence, wisdom, learning, inventor of writing, measurer of time, keeper of divine records. Author of the Book of Thoth, believed to be the fountain of magic and wisdom. The ibis and baboon were sacred to him. His cult center was at Hermopolis. Thoth-Hermes was the mythical writer of the Hermetic books of Roman Egypt.

Wadjet the cobra goddess, protector of Lower Egypt; she was incorporated into the royal diadem.

Wennofer "the good being," one of the designations of Osiris.

Wepwawet "opener of ways," the jackal of Abydos. Guide of souls in the netherworld and protector of tombs.

PROLOGUE:
THE MYTH

Mine is yesterday and I know tomorrow – it means Osiris.
Coffin Texts

Out of the primeval waters rose the hill of creation. On it was the Creator Atum – the All. He uttered his name and then he fashioned a pair: the male Shu – air, and the female Tefnet – moisture. After making himself and his two children, the creator wept. From the tears that fell, mortal men and women came into being. Shu and Tefnet gave birth to a son, Geb – the earth, and a daughter, Nout – the sky. Geb and Nout had two sons and two daughters: Osiris, Seth, Isis, and Nephthys. At the birth of Osiris a voice called out from the heavens announcing that the Lord of All was coming to the light of day.

Seth married his sister Nephthys. Osiris married Isis. They were in love with each other even before they were born and were united in the womb. Seth ruled over the desert, Osiris over the Nile valley. Osiris freed the Egyptians from their brutish manner of life; he showed them how to grow crops, established laws for them, and taught them to worship gods. Isis discovered the way to make bread from wheat and barley. The people of the valley loved this heavenly pair.

So, Seth became envious of Osiris and plotted to murder him. He secretly measured the body of Osiris and had a beautiful chest with exquisite decorations made to Osiris's measurements. He brought it to the banqueting hall, and when guests showed admiration and pleasure at the sight of it, Seth promised that whoever fitted inside it would have it as a gift. They all tried one by one, but no one fitted in. Then Osiris went inside it and lay down. Promptly, Seth slammed the lid and sealed it with lead. He cast the chest into the Nile. The river carried it downstream to the great sea.

Isis was so forlorn that the tears she shed caused the Nile to flood. To this day, the night in summer when the Nile is reported to rise is known in Egypt as the Night of the Teardrop. Isis wandered in a state of distress, asking everyone she met if they had seen the chest, but only when she chanced across some children did she get an answer. They told her the chest was floating towards the great sea. From then on, people revered children for their prophetic powers. Isis sailed beyond the mouth of the river into the vast emptiness of the sea looking for the coffin. It had washed ashore on the Phoenician coast at Byblos and taken root in a tamarisk tree. So beautiful and fragrant was this tree that it was made into a column in the palace of the Phoenician king with the dead hero still locked inside it. After many trials Isis obtained the coffin and brought it back to Egypt. But Seth seized it again and dismembered the body of Osiris into 14 parts. He scattered the severed limbs all over the land and the body of Osiris became one with the soil of Egypt.

The devoted Isis transformed herself into a kite and with her sister Nephthys went searching for all the parts of the body. Wherever she found one, she performed the funerary rites, and that is why there were so many tombs of Osiris all over Egypt. The only part Isis did not find was his male member; for no sooner was it thrown into the river than the lepidotus, phagrus, and oxyrynchus fish ate of it. Ever since, these fish were an abomination to every civilized Egyptian. In its place, Isis fashioned a likeness of it and consecrated the phallus, in honor of which festivals were held in Egypt. She assembled the flesh of Osiris with great love and breathed life into the re-membered body of her husband. From their mysterious, passionate union the child Horus was born at the winter solstice along with the early flowers and blossoms. He was a child of light and the first plants of the season were consecrated to him.

Isis hid the child in the marshes of the north, where the high reeds of the river god protected him from the evil eyes of his murderous uncle. When he grew up, Horus challenged Seth to a mortal battle. Their ceaseless, monumental duel took them before the tribunal of the gods. The gods gave one part of Egypt to Horus and the other to Seth, but then eventually ceded the kingship of Egypt entirely to Horus. Thus was Osiris avenged and righteousness restored to the land.

CHAPTER 1

THE MYTH MAKERS

When heaven had not yet come into existence
When people had not yet come into existence,
When gods had not yet been born
When death had not yet come into existence . . .
                    (Pyramid Texts)

In the beginning was the land, the dry skies, and the hot sands through which meandered the longest river in the world. To the Egyptians, it was simply The River. It burst its banks every year, depositing a fresh layer of silt on the surface of the fields. This was where food was grown and where people lived and worked. The ancient name for Egypt was Kemet, the Black Land – the precious fertile soil along the riverbanks. Here, the Egyptians created, in the words of the German poet Rilke, a "pure, constrained, human, narrow strip of land between river and rock." This unique geographic feature inspired Herodotus to write the often-quoted aphorism that Egypt was a gift of the Nile.

"I was particularly anxious to learn," Herodotus continued,

> why the Nile, at the beginning of the summer solstice begins to rise and continues to increase . . . and why . . . it forthwith retires and contracts its stream, continuing low during the whole of the winter until the summer solstice comes round again. On none of these points could I obtain any information from the inhabitants . . . – they could not tell me what special virtue the Nile has which makes it so opposite in nature to all other streams.[1]

For one thing, the river flowed in the wrong direction, from south to north, unlike any he had heard of. For another, it always flooded once a year at the same time, in the parching summer, when all the other known rivers were at their low point.

Herodotus also recorded the story told him by a scribe who kept the register of the treasures of the temple at Sais: "The fellow did not seem to me to be in earnest when he said that he knew [the sources of the Nile] perfectly well. His story was as follows: . . . There are two hills with sharp conical tops. Midway between them, are the fountains of the Nile, fountains which it is impossible to fathom. Half the water runs northward into Egypt, half to the south." The Nile was a source of mystery: where did it begin and what made it flood?

The river's floods were far from predictable. Nilometers, deep wells that measured the flood rise, were probably invented early in the history of Egypt. Their marks were considered auspicious only if they registered the right number of cubits when the river rose. A low flood and it was one of Seth's curses – drought – bringing with it starvation and the familiar plagues of Egypt. Reliefs on the causeway of king Unas of the Old Kingdom represent emaciated people eating their own lice. A whole literature of lamentation over low floods was recorded in the Middle Kingdom.

The other curse – high water – brought on torrents of water that would break dykes, devastate crops, and destroy villages. Pests in catastrophic numbers would appear in their wake. Seth's weapons were clouds, mists, dust, and darkness. His allies were sandstorms and deadly desert winds.

That is why the Egyptians held Seth in the greatest contempt, observing rituals at various times during the year to keep him from gaining power over the world. Before the flood began, a black pig – the symbol of Seth – was brutally cut into pieces upon a sand altar built on the riverbank. When the desert winds arrived, a clay serpent was hacked with knives.

Small wonder that human fortune was correlated to the rise of the flood. Twelve cubits denoted famine; thirteen, hunger, fourteen – the number of the severed parts of the body of Osiris – cheerfulness; fifteen, complete confidence, and sixteen – delight.[2] The fate of the people and their god were inextricably linked.

The land of Osiris was remarkably ordered. The center of the Egyptian universe was the river. Boats floated downstream with the current and sailed upstream catching the steady north breeze from the Mediterranean. Every morning the sun rose in the eastern desert and set behind the western hills. The desert's edge delineated the sharp boundary between the tranquil world of the fertile plain and the formless wasteland beyond. Melting, colorless horizons set off the clear, bold colors of the valley.

Lush marshlands teeming with fish, waterfowl, and migratory birds stretched on each side of the river, its earthen banks cut straight up and down, slashed away by the rushing waters of the inundation. Crocodiles lay in wait by the reeds and hippopotami lazed in muddy pools. At a short distance from the banks lay the lowland fields, the first to be covered by the inundation. Only the ground that remained above water for the entire year housed villages and public buildings. The dwellings of the dead were in the desert hills. Where the desert began, clusters of bush and sycamore trees surrounded scattered water holes; jackals, lions, and antelopes gathered around them at night.

From June to November the inundation transformed this landscape into a vast sea and the towns became islands. At some places in the Delta it took two days to cross from bank to bank. Boats were the main means of communication. Egyptian ideas about the universe were drawn from this environment.

The lotus became the symbol of the sun because in the evening it closed its blossom and hid its bud so deep under the water that it couldn't be reached by hand. In the morning, the sun's rays drew it to the surface and when it opened its bloom, the petals and perfume radiated from the flower's heart like shafts of sunlight.

Stars were the mantle of the sky goddess. All souls after death became shining stars. They were taken into the embrace of the Great Mother and took part in the never-ending cycles of nature. The imperishable polar star was the guiding light on their ascent to the heavenly heights.

Gods were forces of nature. The sun and the moon were the eyes of the creator. The sun rowed his way across the sky in two boats, Matet – "becoming stronger" – in the morning and Semket – "becoming weaker" – in the evening. The sky goddess swallowed the sun at night and gave birth to him at dawn.

Seth, the adversary, tried to prevent the sun from rising. At dusk he wanted to steal the fading light and plunge the earth into darkness. But Thoth, the god of magic, restored the light by making the moon rise.

Thoth was the heart of the creator and the source of his wisdom. He had a place in the solar boat where he set the course each day. He surveyed the heavens, planned the seasons, and regulated time. Thoth divided the year into three seasons: the inundation (summer), plowing (autumn), and harvest (spring). There were twelve months, each of thirty days. A week was ten days long.

When Thoth fell in love with the beautiful moon goddess he challenged her to a game of draughts. Being crafty, he won the seventieth part of each of her illuminations. From his gains he put together five whole days and added them at the beginning of the year to the three hundred and sixty. In this way, he avoided leap years. The Egyptian year displayed a clear and constant arrangement, running only one-fourth of a day behind the Julian calendar. The five days were celebrated as the birthdays of Osiris, Horus, Seth, Isis, and Nephthys. It was said that the third day, the birthday of Seth, was unlucky and no public business was conducted on that day.

The Nile had acquired the status of divinity – he was Hapi, a portly figure with sagging breasts bearing food offerings. His androgynous form combined the male and female in one. Hapi lived in a cavern from which the fountains of the Nile flowed, and the annual flood was hailed as the arrival of Hapi. The gatekeeper of the flood was Khnum, the ram-headed god of the first cataract, who announced when Hapi's belly began to swell. The river was so beneficent that people believed drinking its waters had a fattening effect and produced excess of flesh. Egyptian priests were baptized in the Nile to acquire their powers. Throughout Egyptian history people who drowned in the Nile were believed blessed because they had drawn closer to the divine realm.

The river suggested ever-flowing, continuous creation as the governing principle of nature. Every part of life was a necessary component of the whole. Sacrifice and death were preconditions of rebirth. It was on the waters of Hapi that Osiris floated until Isis found the pieces and took them to be reunited. Nature required putting together, it obeyed the rules of "Ma'at," a graceful goddess with a feather in her hair. Ma'at held the scales of judgment – the fundamental, unalterable laws that governed the universe and could not be broken. Virtue and salvation depended on her. People had to live by her to be whole and in tune with the world. It was more than a moral obligation, it was a question of maintaining the precarious balance of the essence of life itself.

Immediately after the Nile came the boat (plate 8a). Boats were infinitely more than just a means of transportation. In prehistoric times, boats carrying sacred emblems and fetishes went from village to village as a kind of floating religious ministry that serviced local communities along the river. Through-out the historical period statues of gods were always housed on boats. All gods and goddesses had their own special barges. These vessels of the divine stood on pedestals in the inner sanctum of temples and were carried in processions during festivals. Boats became symbols of celestial transportation for people, too. The souls of those who died traveled to the stars by boat. People were buried with boats that ranged in size from small pottery models found in prehistoric graves to the enormous boats of cedar found near the Great Pyramid of Khufu at Giza.

Gates became a powerful symbol of passage and transition. They per-meated all the literary imagery and were the most important part of temple architecture. Four gates led to the holy of holies. Twelve gates protected the nocturnal regions of the hours of the night. Seven gates preceded the throne of Osiris. In tombs, auspicious images were placed above doorways. Passing through gates invoked the soul's voyage through successive stages of spiritual initiation.

Another deeply engrained belief was the principle of duality. The antagonism of Osiris and Seth marked the constant battle to rescue fertile land from the encroaching sands. The stark contrast between the bleak desert and the abundant river valley inspired the perception of juxtapositions in every sphere of life. Egypt itself was always seen as two lands – the Upper Kingdom and the Delta. Everything existed in paired opposites. Every person had a *ka*, a spiritual double. Duality was implicit in day and night, life and death, the world above the horizon and the netherworld below. The universe operated in dual mode; as above, so below. The place of existence was between two opposite, complementary forces. People's active participation in cosmic affairs was of paramount importance: the survival of the world depended on it.

A New Kingdom story describes how Atum-Ra had tired of his daily routine of rising in the east and setting in the west, always besieged by his enemies. People had neglected their duties to him and he felt old and dejected. He complained of fatigue to Noun, the primeval ocean who set about trying to find him help for his daily duties. Noun persuaded Nout, the sky-goddess, to carry him on her back through the sky each day, but the strain was too much for her and her limbs began to tremble. Ra commanded Shu, the god of the air, to support her belly, but it wasn't enough. When the people saw Ra upon Nout's back and the heavens tremble they bitterly regretted their disregard of him. The next morning they appeared fully armed and ready to do battle against his enemies. Encouraged by their support, Ra decided to forgive them their earlier sins, which he attributed to the serpents' wicked advice. Geb, the earth god, was instructed to keep these dangerous creatures under control, but the struggle was far from over. Thoth was told, from that moment on, to keep a written record of the punishments for Ra's enemies. To ease Thoth's task Ra created the ibis to be Thoth's messengers among people and the baboon to assist him in driving back his enemies.

Gods could choose to appear in animal form. The lone jackal wandering off into the desert horizon was Wepwawet, the Opener of Ways to the other world. The goddess Taweret, a pregnant hippopotamus, was the ultimate image of fertility. The ibis symbolized intelligence because it would never approach or drink poisoned water. The cobra represented the marshes of the north and the vulture the deserts of the south.

Villages were bonded by kinship. Every village had its own heraldic sign. Hieraconpolis worshiped Horus the falcon, and Naqada worshiped Seth the hound. The jackal was the sign of Abydos, the lightning bolt of Min that of Koptos. Min became visible to mortals during rainstorms and his statues were painted black to represent stormy nights. The crocodile, hippopotamus, and scorpion were all local emblems. Plutarch wrote: "Osiris in his great expedition divided his force into many parts and gave them all animal shaped standards, each one of which became sacred and precious to the whole clan of people thus associated."[3] Only the cow, the earthly symbol of the mother goddess, was worshiped everywhere. She was the Great Earth Mother to all the communities along the riverbanks.

Boats that were painted on pottery often had the district emblems displayed on the prows and sterns. The emblems were the first idols. Many later became glyphs in the Egyptian script. Gods' emblems were used as symbols in writing throughout the historic period.

The most important event in the cycle of the seasons was the New Year. A prehistoric palette used for grinding green malachite for makeup, made around 3500 BC, illustrates the rising of the star Sirius in midsummer (figure 1.1). The brightest of all the fixed stars, Sirius appears on the eastern horizon just before sunrise about the time of the summer solstice. This event marked the beginning of the Egyptian year. The palette was shaped as a cow head as well as a dancing figure with upraised arms that terminate with stars. The stars represent the constellation of Orion.

Both Sirius and Orion were related to the Nile flood. The ascent of Sirius during the third week in June heralded the beginning of the Nile's steady rise. By August in Upper Egypt, and September in the north, the river swelled to its full capacity. Then, stars from the constellation of Orion emerged in the night sky after being invisible for seventy days. At this time, the river began to abate. By November, it was back in its bed.

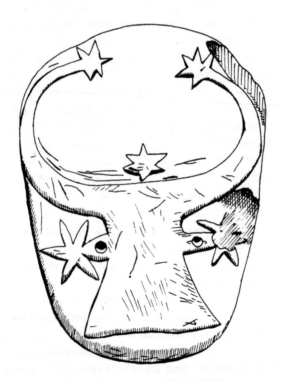

Figure 1.1   Cosmetic palette. Predynastic, ca. 3500–3200 BC

The female figure on the palette in figure 1 may have represented the Great Goddess who symbolized the feminine creative power that conceived and brought forth all living things. She was known by many names and attributes, describing her various personifications and roles. As a mother figure, she protected and nourished all life, hence her association with the cow – "the great feeder of mankind."

The cow appeared as the second oldest deity worshiped by the Egyptians.[4] The first was the star Sirius (the Egyptian Sepdet).[5] Sirius was linked with Isis, "the mistress of the beginning of the year who circles in heaven near the stars of Orion." Were the star and the cow two manifestations of the Great Goddess or were they different deities? The image on this palette seems to merge them into one – the star in heaven and the provider on earth.

The constellation of Orion was linked with Osiris: "He has come as Orion, Osiris has come as Orion," proclaim the Pyramid Texts. Sirius and Orion, Isis and Osiris, inseparable in heaven as on earth, heralded the inundation and the rebirth of life. Their appearance in the sky was a measure of time and a portent of great magnitude. In historic times, both occasions were always marked by celebrations. The cosmetic palette seems to record such a ceremony in the remote prehistoric past, celebrated by ritual dancing.

Aside from female figures, the people of prehistoric Egypt also fashioned figures of cloaked men with long, pointed beards – predecessors of the later ancestor figures. The bearded male may have been the image of the deified founder of the clan, the ancestor-king who acted as a guardian spirit. As such, he may have enjoyed divine status. In historic times, the addition of a beard signified both royalty and divinity. The ancestor figure may have been the male consort of the mother goddess, All-Father like she was All-Mother.

The theory of the ritual sacrifice of the king – father of the clan – has been put forward and discredited time and again. In the first century AD, the Roman geographer Strabo wrote with indignation about the ritual murder of the king performed by the priests in Nubia (Book XVII, 2, 3). It had been associated with the worship of the mother goddess and related to the cycle of the seasons and vegetation rites. Many echoes of the theme can be heard in myths from the Near East and the ancient Mediterranean.

Our only evidence for the presence of this custom in prehistoric Egypt is the story of Osiris itself. It is the dismemberment of the body of Osiris and its scattering all over Egypt that conveys associations with ritual fertilizing of the land. Blood was transubstantiated into water and water enveloped the earth to penetrate it and create new life. The red hue of the river, brought on by oxide sediments during the inundation, to this day is compared with blood. Was this the blood of Osiris? After all, it was the tears of Isis over the slain Osiris that caused the river to swell. They were the divine pair, united since conception in the womb of the sky-goddess, whose mantle was the stars in heaven. The swelling waters of the Nile drowned the land and the sad lamentations of Isis called Osiris out of the heavens. When Orion appeared, the waters began to recede and the first hill rose from the watery abyss, sprouting leaves. Life was reborn from the saturated, black earth. Osiris came back, his flesh as green as the plants in the valley. The mystery of creation was enacted every year since the beginning of time. This was "the form of Him whom one may not name, Osiris of the Mysteries, who springs from the returning waters."

The posthumous conception of the child may have symbolized the magical transfer of the spirit of the dead king into a son and successor. If any common beliefs were shared with the Shillouk people of Sudan still practicing their customs today, Osiris may have been the primeval ancestor who embodied the soul of his people. His violent death would have been necessary to transmit the spirit of the first begetter to the new king – Prime Begetter to Prime Begotten, father to son, one and the same.[6]

Was killing the king ever practiced as magic by some of the ancient clans? Was the king sacrificed to the black earth to ensure a plentiful harvest? What became a mythical, poetic idea in later times might in the beginning have really happened. Ritual came before myth and was the subject of myth. It was the human fate that molded the image of Osiris. People drew consolation and strength from the fate of their god because they recognized themselves in him and because he was always reborn:

> I live, I die: I am Osiris.
> I have entered you, and have reappeared through you . . .
> I have grown in you.
> I have fallen upon my side [died].
> The gods are living from me . . .
> The earth god has hidden me.
> I live, I die, I am barley, I do not perish!
>
> (Coffin Texts)

The pastoral, isolated life of the Nile valley might have continued undisturbed for centuries if not for a sudden turn of events. In the mineral-rich Eastern Desert the Egyptians discovered "white gold," a natural amalgam of gold and silver.[7] This momentous event ended the isolation of the Nile valley forever. Gold attracted visitors from abroad.

Drawn to Egypt by reports of the riches of the small, independent courts, travelers from Sumer arrived. Along with traders came architects and craftsmen, offering their services to the local rulers. It is far from clear who held the monopoly on gold. The ancient name for Naqada was Nubet – "Gold Town." But, at this time, the rival town of Hieraconpolis gained in stature. Its population had increased to such an extent that city walls and a monumental gateway had to be built to protect the inner city. As well as being a defensive structure, the great gate was also a statement of power. Its design and construction were of Sumerian origin, closely resembling the city gate of Uruk in Mesopotamia.

Foreign influences brought dynamic changes. The Sumerians introduced copper to the Nile valley. This led to great technological advances, especially in the making of tools. Copper tools were used for cutting precious metals and stone. Stone architecture was invented. Mining emerged as one of the principal industries. Expeditions were undertaken to the turquoise mines of Sinai and to Nubia to obtain hardwood. Affluence increased and objects of luxury became commonplace.

Prosperity, however, invited rivalry and strife. A new warrior class began to emerge. Many an alliance was probably made and broken as the local rulers competed for prestige and power. Noblemen rose in rank by distinguishing themselves in battle. At first, distinction might have ended with the death of the man who had won it, but patrilineal descent had become increasingly common, creating dynasties. Titles evolved: Scorpion, Lion, Fighting Hawk, Catfish. The people who acquired them became the demigods of national myth.

It was probably at this time that the Great Goddess declined in importance and the male warrior gods rose. The emergence of non-kinship military alliances probably undermined the role of women. Egypt was undergoing a violent transition from tribal to state society.

Among the warring factions the principalities of Hieraconpolis and Naqada emerged as the main protagonists of a great duel. The line of the falcon-king Horus ruled in Hieraconpolis. The line of Seth, a mythical hound, ruled Naqada. These two houses clashed for dominance in a way that could end only by the conquest of one by the other. Thus arose the fateful combat between Horus and Seth. The outcome became the stuff of legend. In a decisive move the followers of Horus defeated those of Seth and the Horus-king asserted himself over all Egypt. Those who disputed the new power were crushed and mastered. War was brought to an end. Trade came to be controlled by a single authority. The future belonged to powerful, absolute monarchs.

CHAPTER 2

ENTER THE
DIVINE KING

After the unification, sacred kingship became the state religion. The first pharaohs used the myth of the ancestral king to claim divine status for themselves. The cosmic battle between Osiris and Seth was now presented as a fight for territory and control of the land. In fact, the entire religious legacy of the prehistoric period was appropriated by the pharaohs of the unification and placed at the service of political expediency.

Some time around 3000 BC, Egypt became one kingdom from the first cataract at Assuan to the Mediterranean Sea. Thinis was chosen as capital because it was midway between Hieraconpolis and the northern territories (its exact location is not known). The final conquest of the north led to the establishment of a new administrative capital at Memphis (modern Mit Rahina), at the place where the Nile forked into the Delta.

Political unification had brought with it remarkable novelties, among them the use of writing. In Egyptian lore, the script had been invented by Thoth and given to people by Osiris. The use of writing to record events in time began Egyptian history. On the oldest king-list from the Fifth Dynasty, the Palermo Stone, it is said that Egypt was unified when Horus gave the throne to the first human king, Men – "the establisher." It is possible that Men, if he existed, merely reunified the two lands, restoring the work of an earlier prince or, even more likely, of an entire royal house. His name has not been corroborated by any finds and it is possible that Men was a designation for either Hor Aha ("fighting hawk") or Narmer ("catfish").

Narmer is known to history from a dedicatory palette found in the temple of Horus at Hieraconpolis. On one side of it Narmer was represented triumphing over enemies with the white crown of Upper Egypt (plate 2) and on the other with the red crown of Lower Egypt. The superhuman figure of pharaoh, splendid and awesome, towered over mortals. He was attended by a sandal-bearer, possibly his son, identified by a rosette – a royal emblem. Narmer was shown in the act of smiting a kneeling captive, probably one of the defeated princes. In front of him, the falcon Horus held the people of the marshlands in bondage. Pharaoh's name was written inside the facade of a palace. The falcon Horus had become the ultimate icon of kings.

The Narmer palette is one of the most important historical documents to survive from the time of unification. It was also one of the finest products of the royal propaganda machine. From now on art in all its forms began to serve the purpose of promoting pharaoh. So did writing and religion. A leap of faith had to go hand in hand with the new regime. Unity could not be achieved through political means alone. Justifying political conquest required the genesis of a new mythology. New epics had to be invented to help transform the prehistoric tribal society into a single state. Tribal myths had to be transfigured into a Great State Myth.

The solution emerged in the person of the divine king. Pharaoh stepped in and took over all the symbols of power. He appropriated the insignia of the lion, the tail of the bull, and the wrap of the leopard – all the emblems of the other chiefs. In this way, he subsumed all the local rulers in his single larger-than-life persona. In the new scheme of things, all local town gods had to become subservient to him. In fact, he had to become a god himself. But how does a political leader become a god? There were no precedents for it on a national scale. Adverse tribal traditions had to be reconciled and people of different lineage united.

One divinity in particular was all-important in Egypt. The omnipresent Great Goddess was worshiped universally all over the land. She had single-handed links to supernatural forces. Promptly, pharaoh became the son and lover of the fertility goddess. His new title, Kamutef – bull of his mother – clearly denotes his sexual role. Two colossal heads of the cow goddess dominate both sides of the Narmer palette. After the invention of writing her name was recorded as Hat-Hor, the "house" or "womb of Horus." Thus, with one stroke of the pen, the divine king appropriated all the attributes of the primeval goddess for himself. It was through assimilating her powers that the male ruler acquired divine status. In fact, the entire cosmogony was construed from the king upward to legitimize his supreme position. Everything was turned upside down; the world was made in reverse order. Creation began with pharaoh and worked its way up to the creator.

Osiris and Isis had become the official father and mother of the divine king at the same time. It was said that their miraculous child was the same as Horus the falcon-king. This way, Horus became not only the legitimate new king, the reincarnation of Osiris, but also the heroic avenger and righteous conqueror of Seth. The discrepancy between the two gods was explained by introducing Horus the Elder and Horus the Younger into the Egyptian pantheon.

But their amalgamation was never successfully resolved and Horus the Child continued to be worshiped in his own right throughout Egyptian history.

Pageant and fanfare promoted the institution of divine kingship. Great ceremonies were an indelible part of the official life of the god-king. They were complex theatrical performances involving large casts and plentiful extras, arranged around the principal player – pharaoh himself. Dramas took place in the principal shrines throughout Egypt to propitiate and overcome the powers of evil that could threaten pharaoh's absolute power. Great officers of state may have impersonated various local gods. Wearing masks and costumes they enacted the ritual of unification, demonstrating that the gods themselves were part of it.

Among the royal pageants, the most remarkable of all was the Heb Sed, a rite of rejuvenation, celebrated by pharaoh thirty years after his accession, when his physical powers began to wane. It was a great occasion for fusing ritual, drama, and magic into one. The purpose of the Heb Sed was to demonstrate pharaoh's physical prowess and to magically invigorate his body in the process. Special rooms, arranged around an open court, were built for the festival. At the appointed time, the court became crowded with clan elders who carried the ancestral tribal emblems. In their presence, pharaoh had to run around a track, four times as ruler of the south and four times as ruler of the north. Then, pharaoh's statue, wrapped in a ceremonial cloak, was buried in the ground. With this act, he symbolically died and was resurrected, once more youthful and recharged with power.

The Heb Sed appears to be a play-acting substitute for the king's ritual death, in which a statue was used as a surrogate for his body. The theme of the Heb Sed is so closely related to the Osiris myth that one cannot help but wonder if it was usurped from Osiris. While sparing his life, the Heb Sed endowed pharaoh with the vestments of divine kingship.

Another popular play was the Conflict of Horus and Seth. In it, the company of characters called "the followers of Horus," possibly the ancestor spirits of the ancient tribes, assisted the king in his struggle with Seth. The battle of Horus and Seth became one of the favorite subjects in Egyptian mythology. It was updated in every historical period. In the Ptolemaic temple at Edfu it was said to have begun during the 363rd year of Ra's rule upon the earth and to have lasted for decades.

Ra had assembled a massive army in Nubia in preparation for an attack on Seth, who had rebelled against him. From a boat floating on the river he directed his troops of footmen, horsemen, and archers. Among them was Horus, who was aching to avenge his father's death. Horus loved an hour of fighting more than a day of feasting and Thoth had given him the power to transform himself into a solar disk with golden wings.

From high up Horus could see Seth hiding in the marshes of the north. He fought him in three battles in the south, six in the north. They changed into crocodiles and hippopotami and fought in the river. One battle was fought on the high sea. But victory eluded both.

At last, Horus challenged Seth to a single combat. Isis decorated her sun's battleship with gold and prayed for his success. Seth had changed into a red hippopotamus at the island of Elephantine and with his voice of thunder raised a storm. High waves tossed about the boat of Horus, but the falcon stood fast by his prow and the golden boat sparkled in the midst of darkness. The duel lasted for three days. In the course of the battle Seth disguised himself as a black pig and wrested Horus's left eye from his head. Horus seized his enemy and pulled off his testicles. At last, Horus took a harpoon and aimed with all his might. He hit the hippopotamus in the head, killing his adversary and avenging his father. Ra restored his eye, which to this day is worn as an amulet against enemies.

The story of the restored eye of Horus demonstrates how the child of Osiris and Isis was assimilated with Horus the king. The symbol of the savior-child was the eye of the sun newly born every year at the winter solstice. It took some imagination to reconcile this part of the myth of Osiris with the mythology of the divine king. This was done through the king's identification with the ancient creator god, whose eyes were the sun and the moon.

In no small part it was the cold, calculated manipulation of ancient mythology by the kings of the unification that produced such jumble and confusion in the historic period. The merging and overlapping of different myths is often difficult to untangle. Much of the unevenness found in Egyptian religion, such as the several competing creation myths, may be due to the great diversity of the prehistoric legacy. But, ultimately, it was the use of myth for political ends that determined how myths were presented after the invention of writing. It is not easy to strip pharaoh of his borrowed plumes and restore them to their proper owners. Put together in everything but meaning, Egyptian religion was riddled with different ideas and contradictions to the very end.

One cannot help but wonder what the people of the Nile valley made of all this. For millennia their lives revolved around the passing of the seasons and cyclical events such as harvests, religious holidays, and local fetes. There was no instrument for measuring time except for the dance of the stars and the inundation of the river. The majority of people were probably not directly involved in the long wars for the control of the valley. Nevertheless, their lives were probably affected at least as much as the lives of the European peasants during the Hundred Years War. After all, it was for their sake that the kings of the unification traveled up and down the valley in the effort to impress upon them that times had irrevocably changed. Theatrical performances, pomp, and ceremony were designed to introduce the new creed to the people, the faith that embraced all other faiths. Did the people really believe that the king was the new Osiris, the living Horus, and that every other deity they worshiped had bowed in allegiance to him? Are they the reason that the apotheosis of pharaoh had to be so literal?

It seems logical that after many years of war and destruction the people of Egypt accepted with open arms the order established by the new regime. The rule of one man was preferable to the rule of petty princes devouring each other. The leadership of the divine ruler came to personify the stability of society. Throughout Egyptian history the word for "state" had not been invented. The idea was implicit in the person of the king and the institution of monarchy.

The men who accomplished the unification of Egypt probably developed their strategy after a long period of trial and error. It was a tribute to their political acumen that Egypt succeeded in remaining unified throughout her long history, overcoming several intervals of fragmentation. The degree of organization and government control they accomplished was astonishing. With no precedents to rely on, they became revolutionary innovators who created new forms in virtually every sphere of life. In a few short centuries they devised a way of life so powerful and enduring that it lasted for more than three thousand years.

CHAPTER 3

ABYDOS

In Egyptian lore Abydos was indelibly linked with Osiris, but the site had a long history of its own, centuries before Osiris first arrived. Abydos was the cemetery of Thinis, the original capital, where the first kings of Egypt were buried. The modern name for the mound is Umm el Kab, "the mother of potsherds." This is where eleven royal tombs were found, including the tombs of Hor-Aha and Narmer. It was through the link to divine kingship that Osiris came to Abydos.

Thinis and its city of the dead were situated in a corner where the Nile makes a bend towards the northeast and then turns west. The mouths of several wadis open up to the east. The largest of them is Wadi Hammamat, a dried riverbed and the ancient line of communication with the Red Sea. From Abydos, several caravan routes lead towards the western oases. The nearest of them is el Kharga, the ancient Oasis Magna. The area of Abydos is at the intersection of two lines, the north–south of the Nile valley and the east–west desert road. In ancient times this was where the peasant population of the Nile valley, the people of Osiris, came in contact with the hunter-gatherer culture of the desert nomads, the followers of Seth. Throughout the historic period Seth remained the god of the desert and the oases. A temple to Seth was built as late as the Persian Period at the oasis of Dakhla.

The idea of political organization and dominance may have come from the desert nomads who were linked to a patriarchal, tribal way of life that depended on exercising sovereignty over a wide area. This was probably where the idea to include the whole of the Nile valley in one kingdom came about.

Many centuries after they were built, the tombs of Umm el Kab became the destination for pilgrims to the land of Osiris. The memory of the first Egyptian kingdom reminded people of the first Egyptian king. The largest among them, the tomb of Djer, was identified as the tomb of Osiris. By then, legend had it that the head of the god had once been buried there.

Figure 3.1   The Ba-bird and the Ka-shadow of the deceased going in and out of the tomb, New Kingdom Book of the Dead, ca. 1250 BC. After Hornung, *Valley of the Kings*, 136

The tombs in the cemetery clustered around a narrow, meandering wadi in the middle of the western hills. Some of the tombs had "exits" on the opposite side of the entrance leading to it.[1] As far back as anyone could remember, this was the dusty path that led to the netherworld. The "exits" presumably pointed the way for the spirits to go back and forth (figure 3.1). The shadows of the dead were as real as people. They needed houses, sustenance, and human contact.

There were three words for the soul in the Egyptian language: *ka*, *ba*, and *akh*. The word *ka*, often translated as "the shadow," described the vital power by which one lived during life and after death. The word *ba* designated the breath of life; it was not bound by death, but flew away from the body like a bird and continued to live in the hereafter. The word *akh* described the shining enlightened spirit in its transcendent state. The phonetic root from which it derived conveyed the basic meaning of "light, brightness, radiance." After death, all souls became *akhu*, enlightened beings. The *akhu* were believed to inhabit the area around the polar star. The feminine form of the word, *akhet*, described the radiant place where the sun rises and sets as well as the land of the blessed dead. In the Old Kingdom, the term *akhet* specified the king's pyramid tomb.

The hereafter was designated by several names. One of them was the Land of the West. The west was the abode of the setting sun, the entry to the realm of night. All cemeteries in Egypt were always placed on the west side of the Nile. Between east and west, the living and the dead, flowed the river, the source of life. The procession from east to west at the time of the funeral was the sailing of the ship of Isis searching for the body of Osiris. The jackal Anubis was the ferryman of souls.

The other name for the netherworld was Duat. The word *duat* was originally written with a star as a reference to the night sky. Somehow in the Egyptian imagination the celestial realm during the night reached into the subterranean world. It was sometimes called "the lower Duat," presumably a sort of lower sky into which the stars disappeared. Duat designated the entry to the inner, non-material world of the spirits. It was a boundary, a threshold that led to the space of the imaginary. Duat was where the gods lived.

Nowhere did the Egyptian imagination reign as free as in the descriptions of the Duat. It was envisioned as many things: a dusky golden staircase guarded by a jackal, a vast ocean through which two fishes guided the boat of the sun, a cavernous nocturnal world filled with danger through which the otherworldly Nile flowed like a faint stream of consciousness, and even as the sleeping human body of the Great Mother. In the New Kingdom, inspired visions of this imaginary world were described in the Books of the Afterlife.

The distance between gods and mortals was overcome in death. Death was the fulfillment of life, the transcendence of the gulf between the two worlds. Through dying, people partook in the essence of the divine. They could conquer death and rise again because divine life always rises again. The Coffin Texts said: "I am Thoth, I am Ra in his ascent, I am Kheper who came forth from himself." The dead were believed to possess some of the power that enabled gods to triumph over death.

A note of optimism was struck in this view of the fate of human beings. There was a sense that the human and the divine came very close together as two aspects of the same integral experience. Perhaps that is why to the modern mind Egyptian culture appears to be necrocentric – the ancient Egyptians speak to us from their tombs.

The Egyptian cosmology was without an apocalypse, without the end of time. Time was not moving towards an eternal consummation, it simply *was*.[2] It was cyclical and ever repeating. The cycles of decay and renewal occurred in indefinite time, so that, with respect to human observation, this world had neither a beginning nor an end. Eternity was outside time. This idea of permanence and continuity caused people to attempt to preserve their bodies forever. They believed that the soul revivified the body and that the full, embodied person retained their life. St. Augustine wrote: "The Egyptians alone believe in the resurrection, as they carefully preserve their bodies. They have a custom of drying up their bodies and making them as durable as brass." Cremation was abhorrent and reserved for evildoers who were thereby rendered non-existent.

17

This emphatic denial of death led to the development of complex rituals designed to maintain the unity and integrity of a person, including their body. Tombs were eternal homes designed to provide all the material support of life and were often packed like treasure chests. That is why they were so attractive to tomb robbers. Food, furniture, and even favorite pets accompanied the dead. Tombs were eternal sanctuaries, hence their monumentality.

The crown of all the earthly provisions was the mummified body. The word for mummy, *sah*, also meant "nobility, dignity." It was the name of the constellation of Orion – the spirit of Osiris – and also meant "spirit, soul." It denoted the elevated sphere of existence to which the deceased was initiated in the process of embalming. The rejoining of the limbs of Osiris furnished the mythical precedent and became the model for overcoming death. Mummification was more than the mere preservation of the corpse; by substituting perishable substances with everlasting ones, the body was transfigured and "filled with magic." It became "an Osiris" (plate 5).

The mode of embalming is described by Herodotus:

> They take first a crooked piece of iron, and with it draw out the brain through the nostrils, thus getting rid of a portion, while the skull is cleared of the rest by rinsing with drugs; next they make a cut along the flank with a sharp Ethiopian stone (either black flint or Ethiopian agate), and take out the whole contents of the abdomen, which they then cleanse, washing it thoroughly with palm wine, and again frequently with an infusion of pounded aromatics. After this they fill the cavity with the purest bruised myrrh, with cassia, and every other sort of spicery except frankincense, and sew up the opening. Then the body is placed in natrium for *seventy* days, and covered entirely over. After the expiration of that space of time, which must not be exceeded, the body is washed and wrapped round, from head to foot, with bandages of fine linen cloth, smeared over with gum . . . and in this state given back to the relations.[3]

The bandages were often inscribed with spells from the Book of the Dead.

During the seventy days in which the deceased's body underwent mummification – the same time that the constellation of Orion "disappeared" from the summer skies – the departed soul lay unconscious in the Duat. During that time, Osiris–Orion was said to regenerate in the netherworld. There, every soul awaited, like Osiris, the moment at which the scattered organs would be gathered together. Only within the reconstituted body could the soul be resurrected.

Numerous rites were performed on the mummy during the burial. There were no boundaries between the two worlds that could not be bridged in endless rituals of reciprocity. Performing the rite was more important than knowing the story behind it. In fact, secrecy contributed to the desired magical effect of the ritual. Through ritual, the difference between life and death, mortals and immortals was transcended. Rituals were designed to prevent a second death – oblivion.

Spells and incantations were recited to bring the dead out into the day. "Stepping forth into Daylight" was the name of the Egyptian Book of the Dead. The latter may be the only book written entirely for a dead audience. The afterlife was seen as the continuation of life. In death people went on doing everything they had done on earth. There was even a strong conviction that erotic powers could help revive the dead. Among tomb offerings it is not unusual to find phalluses or concubine figures. A New Kingdom funerary papyrus contains the following spell:

> A spell for going out into the day,
> Of coming and going in the realms of the dead,
> Of entering the field of reeds . . .
> Having power there,
> Being glorious there,
> Plowing there and reaping,
> Eating there, drinking there, making love there,
> Doing everything that used to be done on earth.

All of the required provisions increased the cost of a proper funeral to a formidable degree. The average Egyptian of the pharaonic period had a life expectancy of 30–6 years, was poor, illiterate, and could not afford a lavish burial. As a consequence, the vast majority of Egyptian burials were silent and invisible. Even the poor, however, made their bids for eternal life. Pilgrimage to sacred sites and ritual offerings in temples ensured that their voices were heard in the halls of eternity. The temple of Khenti Amentiu in Abydos was among their prime destinations.

The designation Khenti Amentiu meant "foremost of the Land of the West." The god, represented as a jackal, was the guardian of the netherworld. He was known by another name, Wepwawet – "the opener of ways" – an appropriate name for a god who guided spirits to the Duat. To this day, the Fellahin claim that by following a jackal's footprints in the desert they can find water. His third name, Anubis, designated him as the god of embalming. The jackal was the heraldic sign of Abydos in prehistoric times and it is to this god that the earliest temple there was dedicated.

Anubis played an important part in the myth of Osiris; according to Plutarch, he was the son of Osiris. It was during her mourning that Isis was told that her sister Nephthys fell in love with Osiris and tricked him into her bed. A garland Osiris left behind was proof of the truth of the story. Rumor had

19

it that Nephthys had become pregnant from the occasion, but fearing her husband Seth, she left the boy exposed after birth. Wild dogs found the child and saved him. When Isis discovered this, she searched out her nephew, gave him the name Anubis, and reared him as her own. From then on he watched over Isis as mortal dogs do over people.

Anubis helped Isis restore the body of Osiris by wrapping it in mummy bandages. This act made him indispensable for human beings who hoped that he would restore their bodies as well. At funerals, the priests who performed the funerary rites wore jackal masks to show that they were Anubis's representatives on earth.

At some distance from the royal tombs at Um el Kab, on the edge of the fertile fields, the dead pharaohs possessed another "house" where they continued to live in the form of statues. These were "houses for the *ka*," the shadows. The cult of deceased kings was maintained long after their death.

The temple of Abydos was built in front of the royal "*ka* houses," on the processional way that led through a gate from the cultivated land to the royal cemetery in the desert. The temple's outside court for offerings was enlarged several times, as the site became more popular. The only known representation of Khufu (the Greek Cheops), the builder of the Great Pyramid at Giza, was an ivory statuette dedicated at Abydos.

Other offerings revealed a popular piety quite unconcerned with the royal dead. A great number of figurines, some of crude workmanship, represented monkeys, hippopotami, crocodiles, birds, and children. These figurines were objects of magic designed to inspire divine intervention. Although it is far from clear what the numerous figures meant to the people who brought them along, many of them, particularly those of children, seem to be related to fertility and birth. The frog and the hippopotamus later became deities associated with fertility. It is still widely believed in Egypt that the dead can intervene on behalf of the living to help secure progeny. The belief stems from the conviction that the dead inhabit the same world as the gods.

Under Djoser of the Third Dynasty, the royal tomb with its accompanying cult buildings was transferred to Saqqara, the necropolis of Memphis. One would have expected Abydos to decline in importance and become nothing but a distant memory. But, although kings of the Old Kingdom were now buried at Saqqara and Giza, they continued to build additional "*ka* houses" in Abydos. The royal cult persisted at the temple of Khenti Amentiu and it was still believed that the spirits of deceased kings became glorified in accordance with the ancient ritual at Abydos.

The continuing importance of Abydos was confirmed by royal decrees of tax exemption granted to the temple by Neferirkara of the Fifth Dynasty and Tety of the Sixth. They put up stellae on the processional way leading to the royal cemetery, specifying that priests and bondmen of the temple were freed from duties to the king except in continuing to maintain the royal cult. Thus, although the actual burial of the king took place in the north, the passage to eternity still proceeded through the gateway of Abydos.

When Osiris arrived at Abydos some time at the end of the Fifth Dynasty, he came through the link with kingship. Until now, immortality had been confined to the divine king. Ordinary Egyptians, their piety developed through the royal cult, now began to seek immortality for themselves. Through the identification of Osiris with the dead king they were given in Abydos the bridge they needed.

After the arrival of Osiris at Abydos, the ancient royal ritual was remade to suit his myth. Osiris was identified with Khenti Amentiu and "Foremost of the Land of the West" became one of his designations. Finally, the festivities at Abydos became dedicated to Osiris rather than to the dead king. The so-called Mysteries of Osiris, well documented from the Middle Kingdom on, were modeled on the ancient royal ritual. In this way, from the most ancient home of the first kings of Egypt streamed the great faith that for thousands of years nourished a whole nation with a belief in another world.

CHAPTER 4

PYRAMID BUILDERS

The Old Kingdom, the rule of Dynasties III–VI (2686–2181 BC), represented the greatest consolidation of monolithic power that Egypt experienced in its long history. There was no historical or political division between the first two dynasties and the latter four. The term Old Kingdom was coined in the nineteenth century to describe the progress of monumental architecture that began in Dynasty III.

The name for the new capital was Ineb Hedj – "white wall." It was built at the northernmost point of the Nile, before it branched out into the Delta. Herodotus was told that the pharaohs diverted the course of the river by a dyke to create more land for the new city. "To this day, the elbow which the Nile forms at the point where it is forced aside into the new channel is guarded with the greatest care . . . and strengthened every year; for if the river was to burst out at this place and pour over the mound, there would be danger of Memphis being completely overwhelmed by the flood." The location of the original dyke is not known. Over the millennia silting continued to displace the head of the Delta; between the Old Kingdom and the Arab conquest it had moved 20 kilometers north.

Memphis continued to play a central role throughout Egypt's long history. The emergence of other capitals, such as Thebes in the New Kingdom, did not diminish its importance. The city's position at the junction of Upper and Lower Egypt ensured its continued viability. The commercial weight of Memphis was reinforced during the Late Period, when Nekau II (610–595 BC) excavated a canal between the Nile valley and the Red Sea, using an old channel of the Nile. The canal proved difficult to maintain; the Persian king Darius, the Roman emperor Trajan, and the Arab conqueror of Egypt Amr Ibn el-As restored it. It was only with the founding of Alexandria in 332 BC that Memphis declined.

The Greek word *Memphis* derived from the Egyptian *Men-Nefer-Pepy* ("the beautiful monument of Pepy"), the name of the pyramid of Pepy II, built three hundred years after the city's original foundation. By then, royal palaces and pyramids had moved south, away from the noise and squalor of the crowded city. The southern quarters were linked with public buildings in the north by the expanding settlements and the capital in its entirety became known as Men-Nefer.

For the pharaohs, conquering the Delta also meant draining the swamps, cutting down the thickets, and setting up irrigation projects. They began a vast program of reclaiming land from the marshes, implemented for more than two thousand years and completed only during the rule of the Ptolemaic kings. By the Old Kingdom, Egypt was made up of forty-two districts or provinces. They covered the area of approximately 25 miles along the riverbanks; in the Delta they followed the branches of the Nile. The principal districts of Egypt endured throughout her long history. Every time the unified Egyptian state fell apart, power reverted to the provinces.

Monumental architecture appeared during the reign of Djoser (2667–2648 BC). The Egyptians viewed Djoser, whose name meant "sacred, holy," as the creator of a new era. He was the first to introduce a long period of prosperity and peace, thus far unequaled in the experience of the Two Lands. During his reign, state resources could for the first time be organized on a scale that permitted monumental public works.

The building of Djoser's funerary monument and its surrounding structures, the step pyramid of Saqqara (plate 1a), required the employment of thousands of workers and craftsmen. It provided extra work and additional income for the farmers during the slow months of the inundation. At this season the river came to the very edge of the necropolis, facilitating the transport of building materials by boat (plate 1b). The farmers probably welcomed the chance of new employment. Graffiti written on some of the stone blocks, praising one gang of workmen or disparaging another, generally revealed an attitude of loyalty to the king.

The scheme seemed to work and building on a monumental scale became the prerogative of the ruling elite for several more generations. The arts of architecture, sculpture, and relief advanced to a remarkable degree. Other professions also proliferated and for the first time individuals other than the king became known to history.

Djoser's architect Imhotep was revered as a great master, sage, and healer. The discovery of a statue base in 1926, inscribed with the names and titles of Imhotep, dispelled any doubts that he was a historical figure. From the Twenty-sixth Dynasty on, Imhotep was worshiped as a god in his own right, with temples and priests serving in them. The Greeks identified him with Asclepius. His fame endured through the Middle Ages and the Renaissance in Europe and he was even credited with having been the spiritual father of

Freemasonry. The center of Imhotep's worship was in Memphis; his tomb presumably still lies under the sands of Saqqara.

The patron god of Memphis was Ptah, the maker of all visible forms and the protector of craftsmen and artisans. Legend had it that Men, the first king of Egypt, built the temple of Ptah. The god's origins are obscure. He seems to be associated with the kings of the First Dynasty and may have come with them from Upper Egypt. Like Atum-Ra, he was also a creator-god, described as "the fashioner of the earth who made all gods, men and animals, all lands and shores of the ocean."

The temple of Ptah was the heart of ancient Memphis. It had been generously patronized during the First and Second Dynasties. From the First Dynasty on, the bull Apis was kept in a stall within the temple precinct, probably as the king's power animal. In time, the cults of Apis, Ptah, and Osiris merged and Apis was seen as the divine incarnation (*ka*) of Ptah. In the Late Period the designation of the temple *hekaptah* – "the domain of the *ka* of Ptah" – was used as one of the names for the capital. From this word derived the Greek *aigyptos* – Egypt.

After death the bulls were mummified and buried with pomp like Osiris and their bandages inscribed with the title of Osiris-Apis. In time, their mummies had become so many that in the New Kingdom vast underground galleries had to be excavated for them at Saqqara. The Greeks called this underground structure the Sarapeum, after Osiris-Apis – the Greek Sarapis. Plutarch mentioned that "certain bronze gates" at Memphis opened with a heavy and harsh grating sound whenever they buried Apis.[1]

The title of the High Priest of Ptah was one of the most powerful of all the religious titles and nearest to the concept of pontiff that Egypt ever knew. The High Priest was the supreme director of the armies of builders, sculptors, potters, woodcarvers, and metal smiths of all kinds. His role in planning royal tombs and temples was crucial. Often, the king's eldest son was installed in this office.

The priesthood played a crucial part in the religious and political life of the country. The High Priests of Amun were designated as First Prophets, those of Ra as Great Seers, those of Ptah as Directors of Craftsmen, and those of Thoth as Greatest of the Five. All of them communicated the messages of their respective gods through oracular consultations. Small wonder that kings had to pay great attention to the clergy. In the Middle Kingdom we have records of kings being chosen to rule by divine oracles.

By the time the temple of Kom Ombo was built in the Ptolemaic Period, a special corridor was provided underground to enable the priests to approach the niche with the divine statue from the back, invisible to visitors. From there, standing behind a thin wall, they could hear and answer questions and petitions. The temple of Amun in the Siwa Oasis, consulted by Alexander the Great himself, had a similar room above the sanctuary, approached by a ladder from the back. Lying on their bellies above the ceiling the priests could hear the questions directed to the god's statue. Answers were then provided on scrolls handed out to the supplicants in another chamber.

The proximity of Heliopolis – City of the Sun – to Memphis played an important part in the development of religion. The hold of the priesthood of Ra over the king grew progressively during the Old Kingdom. By the Fourth Dynasty, the worship of the sun emerged as the principal royal cult. Djed-ef-ra was the first to adopt the title Son of Ra. So powerful was the sun-cult that even the divine king did not dare usurp it for himself and was content to remain merely the son of the sun god. Instead, the verb for sunrise, "to appear in glory," was used to mark the appearance of pharaoh on state occasions.

As the priests of Heliopolis rose in power, the idea of the sun began to dominate Egyptian models of thought. Gods and dead kings were still identified with stars, but the worship of the sun changed the concept of the afterlife. The creation of the true pyramid went hand in hand with the rise of the solar cult. The true pyramid embodied the idea of perfection of the primeval hill illuminated by sunlight streaming down from heaven.

The Egyptian word for pyramid was *mer*. The word "pyramid" was derived from the Greek *pyramis*, the original meaning of which is uncertain. The discovery of the true pyramid in monumental architecture was gradual. The first pyramid at Maidum, built by either Huni (2637–2613 BC) or Snofru (2613–2589 BC) in the late Third/early Fourth Dynasty, collapsed because its angle was too steep. It was later restored during the Middle Kingdom, the earliest example of monument conservation.

Snofru built two more pyramids at Dahshur. Designated by the same name, Epiphany of Snofru, they were planned as related funerary complexes and built simultaneously. The angle of one was too steep at the outset and half way, once this had been realized, a shallower angle was applied to the rising walls. As a result, the walls ended up with a bent angle. The other pyramid was built with a shallower angle from the start and thus had perfectly straight walls; it became the prototype for the three pyramids at Giza. It still remains uncertain in which of the two pyramids Snofru was actually buried.

Of the three pyramids at Giza, the oldest one was the Great Pyramid of Khufu. It was designated by the name Horizon of Khufu. Possibly led by the desire to outdo all his predecessors, Khufu (2589–2566 BC) set out to make the greatest building ever known to man. He seems to have overextended himself and even later generations did not remember him kindly. Stories of his cruelty still circulated in Giza at the time of Herodotus' visit and he reported tales that Khufu had even sold his daughter to obtain stone for his building.

Indeed, stone was what Khufu needed most of all. The Great Pyramid contained 6 million tons of stone, brought from near-by quarries, finely cut and fitted into place course by course. Some 2.3 million blocks were cut for the structure.[2] When finished, it rose 149 meters in height, the tallest building in the world until the Eiffel Tower was constructed. Herodotus tells us that it took twenty years to make, preceded by ten more for the gigantic ramp necessary for transporting the stones to the building site. Herodotus judged the ramp to be "not much inferior to the pyramid itself, 5 furlongs in length, 10 fathoms wide and in height 8 fathoms, built of polished stone and covered with carvings of animals."[3] The ramp is now buried under the modern village of Nazlet es-Seman.

The Great Pyramid was permeated by the idea of the absolute. Its meaning was related to divine kingship and the cosmic order – the king was the living son of that order and a mediator between people and gods. He was at the nexus of supernatural relationships that provided the sacred order of things. Through him, society acquired meaning and purpose and people found prescriptions for a good life and a meaning for their existence.

The control of masses of men engaged in hard, demanding, and often highly skilled work called for organizational skills of an exceptional order. The internal mathematics of pyramid building were immensely complex. Despite the improvisational element in discovering the intricacies of their construction, the builders seem to have been not only in command, but also intensely conscious of the challenges presented by mass and quantity. Particularly impressive was the skillful employment of saw-tooth edging applied to the blocks in the inner corridor of Khufu's pyramid, preventing them from splaying out under the tremendous weight pressing down upon them. Even when there was a major disaster, such as during the collapse of the Maidum pyramid, the lessons were quickly learned. The architects seem to have been aware of the mathematical properties now represented by the letter π. Possibly obtained from practical experience, this knowledge had a profound influence on their ability to design and build complex structures. Monumentality, elegance of line, and minimal decoration were among the glories of this age.

The Great Pyramid of Khufu was surrounded by subsidiary pyramids for his queens and by large pits for boat burials. Two wooden boats were buried with the king to transport him to the "imperishable stars of the northern sky." One of these dismantled cedar vessels has been excavated and restored with great attention. Its elegant proportions and refined craftsmanship matched the best accomplishments of the age. So did the size; until today, no larger boat of its kind has sailed the Nile. In its day, it must have been a vivid advertisement for imperial might. Its most remarkable feature was that every plank was sewn rather than nailed or riveted. The technique of sewing craft was immensely

Figure 4.1 The Great Sphinx, folio page of Napoleon Bonaparte's "*Descriptions de l'Egypte*" published in Paris in 1822

ancient; it is still practiced in the remote reaches of the coast of Oman, where it may have originated. If the Predynastic Sumerian boats sailing from the Persian Gulf were sewn boats, it would have been possible to disassemble them, carry them overland if the need arose, and sew them together again. The boat of Khufu preserved some of the ancient technology that may have played a part in the prehistoric trade routes.

In the next two generations after Khufu two more pyramids were added on the Giza plateau which, along with the gigantic sculpture of the sphinx, created a spectacular effect. Although the second pyramid of Khafra (the Greek Chephren, 2558–2532 BC) was slightly smaller than its predecessor, it was built on higher ground and appears equally immense. The Great Sphinx was carved from living rock, shaped artificially into a lion's body. The colossal face of Khafra modeled in granite was then attached to the body. The king was represented as a lion warding off inimical forces, a powerful guardian of his own pyramid complex (figure 4.1).

Aside from its monumental size, the sphinx also radiated an undeniable monumentality of vision. It had what all great art has: presence. It was stone but it seemed sentient. The poet Rilke wrote that it had "silently and forever set the human face to be weighed on the scale of the stars." Already in the Old Kingdom the Egyptians venerated the sphinx as a god and a cult temple for offerings was built in front of his paws. So forceful was the otherworldly radiance of this statue that in the Middle Ages, long after its meaning had been forgotten, it mortally offended a fervent adherent of Sufism named Mohammed Said ed-Dahr. According to several medieval Arab authors, he thought the statue sacrilegious and proceeded to deface it, smashing the nose in AD 1378. This, he believed, prevented the sphinx from breathing and effectively "suffocated" the spirit within it.

With the addition of the third pyramid of Menkaura (2532–2503 BC) the sight of Giza was complete. It was a heroic vision, the perfect, geometric shapes and the human-faced lion towering above the sands in the blazing sun. Proclaimed one of the seven wonders of the ancient world, the only one still standing today, Giza has continued to inspire awe throughout the ages. Gustave Flaubert, one of the first European writers to catch the fever of Egyptomania that spread in Europe after Napoleon's expedition to Egypt, visited Giza in the winter of 1849–50. He described his experience: "The sand, the pyramids, the sphinx, all gray and bathed in rosy light, the sky perfectly blue, eagles slowly wheeling and gliding around the tips of the pyramids. We stop at the sphinx, it fixes us with a terrifying stare . . . I am afraid of becoming giddy and try to control my emotions. We walk around the pyramids, right at their feet."[4]

For the Egyptians, Giza became another entry to the netherworld, like Abydos before it. Some time during the New Kingdom an Osiris shaft was excavated deep under the Giza plateau, half way under the causeway between the Sphinx temple and the pyramid of Khafra. The shaft descended to an underground island surrounded by crystal-clear water on which lay the mythical sarcophagus of Osiris, made of solid stone. The sarcophagus was inscribed with the word *per* – "house."

It is difficult to imagine that this obscure place that can be accessed only by climbing down 100-foot ladders in pitch darkness pierced only by the sounds of dripping water was visited with any frequency. It was the god's mythical tomb, literally hidden under the earth. By the time Herodotus visited the pyramids, its location had been forgotten. Perhaps some of the older guides who took the Greek traveler around remembered hearing about it – Herodotus wrote that there were underground vaults at Giza "surrounded by water introduced from the Nile by a canal."[5] But he never saw the place and believed that it was the tomb of Khufu – Cheops.

In the Old Kingdom the pyramid complexes were furnished with sculpture and relief from the royal workshops. Royal cults were meant to be perpetuated for all eternity. The king's artists had mastered the technique of working in stone to such perfection that some of their accomplishments have not been equaled since in Egyptian art. All the temples and causeways around the pyramids were decorated with statues and reliefs that immortalized the king's presence in the hereafter.

The Giza monuments had used up vast resources and the ambitions of Khufu, Khafra, and Menkaura had to be tamed. After the Fourth Dynasty, the size of royal pyramids and accompanying monuments became much smaller and more manageable. The inner chambers were now decorated with religious texts that seem to have taken precedence over size. One of the consequences of the immense organization and labor needed for the pyramids was the recruitment and training of hosts of artists and craftsmen. Some time during the Fourth Dynasty, when the king no longer absorbed virtually all the available labor, a pool of highly skilled artists turned to the nobles and all other prosperous people to decorate their private monuments.

The gradual intrusion of ordinary folk into the world of the Great Ones began in the Fourth Dynasty, increased in the Fifth, and became characteristic of the Sixth. All those who could afford it now began building funerary monuments for themselves. They too wanted to enjoy a glorious eternity once reserved for the king and his family. Women mostly shared tombs with their husbands, but some had their own tombs.

The king acknowledged this change, giving his favorite courtiers "houses for millions of years." They were tombs intended to serve as estates in the hereafter, much like the lands, herds, and servants bestowed in life. Reliefs in private tombs display a great variety and freedom of subject matter. The images of daily life that the deceased hoped to immortalize were a joyous hymn to life and the spirit of existence. It was also within private tombs that writing took its first steps toward literature.

When writing first appeared in Egypt, its use was limited to the brief notations designed to identify a person, a place, or a possession. As its use steadily increased, writing was employed to enumerate the foods, ointments, and textiles dedicated in the private tombs. Somewhat prosaically, the first literary compositions took the form of offering lists carved on the walls of Old Kingdom tombs. The offering lists eventually grew to enormous length, until an inventive mind realized that a short prayer for offerings would be an effective substitute.[6]

In a similar development, the ever-longer lists of people's ranks and titles eventually gave birth to the genre of autobiography. During the Fifth Dynasty, both the prayer and the autobiography acquired their essential features. Although subject to some literary elaboration, the prayer was essentially part of the cult of the dead and not literary in the full sense. The autobiography, however, became a truly literary product. Its aim was the same as that of the self-portrait in sculpture and relief: to immortalize the likeness of an individual in the face of eternity. Thus, it became increasingly self-laudatory, just like the portrait became a combination of the realistic and the idealized (plate 3). Eventually, the autobiography led to the development of the so-called "instructions in wisdom," mostly collections of maxims of upper-class Egyptians that set down a code of behavior befitting a gentleman of the Old Kingdom.

Kings had no autobiographies. Their lives were public, stylized, and remote. Literary imagination took wing only in the realm of the afterlife. The Pyramid Texts carved in stone on the inner walls of the late Fifth and Sixth Dynasty pyramids were the first literary formulations of the Egyptian cosmogony. They were as important to the history of Egypt as the Vedic texts were to the history of the Aryan language and culture. They were the oldest corpus of religious writings, comprising a group of 759 chapters of different length. Some scholars consider them to be a collection of disparate documents, whereas others see them as magical texts recited during a pharaoh's burial. It is beyond doubt that the texts had their roots in the religion of prehistoric Egypt, arranged to suit the structured state of the Old Kingdom monarchs. It is also evident that some texts were recited during the king's burial – spells were generally introduced with the phrase "recitation."

The Pyramid Texts were instrumental in facilitating the king's transfiguration. Spoken and written words had become ideal vehicles for crossing the distance between the real and mythical worlds. Reciting religious texts during the funeral and writing them inside the tomb ensured that they were heard, seen, and present in the hereafter. They were esoteric by nature, not meant to be seen by the eyes of mortals, but written for the gods who lived in the Duat. Their mere presence in the tomb had an exonerating effect on the dead. Their magic invoked the timeless world of the primeval period.

The pyramid itself, the "radiant place of the king," was seen as a physical expression of the otherworldly realm, the king's personal Duat.[7] The pure, geometric shape had become the architectural equivalent of the cosmic perfection. The proportions suggested the majestic, immutable existence to which the king would ascend. The orientation of the pyramids and the chambers inside them reflected the movement of the sun and the stars. Texts were distributed to illustrate the spiritual journey in the hereafter. The soul descended into the netherworld in the west, came to rest in the sarcophagus chamber – "the most secret place" – and rose with the sun in the east. Following the texts, the reader (the spirit of the king) moved through the rooms, adding the dimension of space to their meaning.

The "most secret place" was where Osiris resided before he came back. Every pyramid had an underground chamber that evoked Osiris's hidden abode under the earth. In it, the king was buried Osiris-like to obtain Osiris's power of resurrection. Even when the royal mummy was laid to rest in a different chamber, such as in the Great Pyramid of Khufu, an underground pit was excavated for the purpose of ritual and magic. The Osiris shaft built under the causeway behind the Great Sphinx embodied this idea quite literally. The fact that it was hidden from view made its power all the more vibrant.

Later in the Old Kingdom, ordinary people began using some of the royal Pyramid Texts in their own houses of eternity. The so-called Coffin Texts, known from wooden coffins of the Middle Kingdom, had extensive borrowings from the Pyramid Texts. From the New Kingdom on, the Coffin Texts were reused in the book of Stepping forth into Daylight, better known as the Book of the Dead. Many were written on temple walls. Thus, verses from the Pyramid Texts were handed down through the entire Egyptian history in one form or another, added to or subtracted from, modified or glossed over, reinterpreted or illustrated. As the oldest religious texts, they were always vested with great sanctity and mystical portent.

In the Pyramid Texts we encounter for the first time the plethora of deities that made up the divine realm of ancient Egypt. Clustered around the king, they served as his assistants in the afterlife. The names of the gods were always descriptive; they were epithets explaining their nature: Atum was "the undifferentiated one," Horus "the distant one," Amun "the hidden one." The moon-god Khonsu was "the one who travels across the sky," the lioness Sakhmet "the powerful one." Gods' names were taboo names, and to know them was dangerous, even sacrilegious. Pious people refrained from mentioning them, preferring descriptive designations. The name was the key to the being and to know the name would enable one to control the being.

It was said in a New Kingdom story that only Isis knew the secret name of Ra. She had envied Ra his power over all creatures and plotted to obtain it. Ra's dominion lay in the fact that he alone knew his secret name. Isis fashioned a snake of clay and mixed it with Ra's spittle so that the poison would contain Ra's own divine substance and his body would have no defense against it. She breathed life into it and the snake struck its fangs into the flesh of the father of the gods. The cry of rage that escaped from Ra shook the heavens and earth. The poison spread throughout his body, his limbs began to shake, and his teeth chattered. Isis offered to heal him if he would reveal his secret name to her. Ra's secret name was his most carefully guarded possession and he was reluctant to reveal it: "I am light and I am darkness, I am the maker of the hours, the creator of days . . . I am Khepri in the morning, Ra at noontime, and Atum in the evening." But Isis wanted to know his secret name, for only those whose names she knew could be

31

Figure 4.2   The sky goddess Nout, Late Period sarcophagus, ca. 660 BC. After Hornung, *Valley of the Kings*, 90

healed by her magic. Ra whispered it to her, she healed him, and her power became even greater. But she kept it to herself and concealed Ra's secret name from gods and mortals to this day. Aside from this secret name, Ra had seventy-five other names. They were attributes describing the manifold aspects of his divinity. Each name was a god in his own right. Isis was called "the myriad-named." The number of her names was not merely large but infinite.

The descriptive nature of gods' names and ultimately of the gods themselves was the main reason why gods in Egypt exchanged attributes so seamlessly. Different gods could be combined to designate compound beings, such as Ra-Atum or Ptah-Sokar-Osiris, thus being two-in-one or three-in-one. If gods were merely different designations of the divine, god could be one and the other, One and Many.[8] The Egyptians did not perceive a discrepancy between the great god who was seemingly one and the myriad of gods. Ultimately, all gods were reflections of the same godly essence that was non-definable and mystical. The Hermetic writings of Roman Egypt said: "To understand god is difficult; to speak of god impossible. For the material cannot express the non-material; the imperfect cannot comprehend the perfect."[9]

Like the other gods, it was in the Pyramid Texts that Osiris was first mentioned in writing. At the outset, his position was not as overwhelmingly dominating as it was later to become. He was merely one of the gods that surrounded the king and his role was confined to being identified with the dead king: "Hail Horus! This king is Osiris!"

More often, the king was simply called Osiris Unas, Osiris Tety, or Osiris Pepy. This implied that when the king died, he became one with Osiris: "How great are you, O king. Thy name is raised to [that of] Osiris." With this identification, the stamp of kingship was doubly impressed on the god's personality and Osiris became king of the dead.

As a star, Osiris was related to Orion and the inundation. A number of verses linked him to the fertilizing waters of the Nile: "recitation: your water belongs to you, the moisture that came forth from the god, the effusion that came forth from Osiris." The king was told to wash his hands "in this fresh water which thy father Osiris has given thee." The ultimate source of sacerdotal power was the life-giving Nile whose waters rose through the sacrifice of the god.

The first representation of Osiris was found on a relief of king Djed-ka-ra Isesi of the Fifth Dynasty. Osiris was represented as a man with a curled beard and divine wig in the manner of traditional ancestor figures. He was only one in a long procession of deities around the king and did not stand out in any way.

The name of Osiris was written with the signs for the eye and the throne. The name of Isis was also written with the sign for the throne. Isis was the personification of the seat of power – she caused the one enthroned upon her to become king. Even more than that, the spelling of the names of Osiris and Isis demonstrates that they were inexorably linked. They were an age-old pair, two aspects of the same primal being. In scholarship it is still debated whether the concept of the throne played a part in writing the name of the god. Who came first, the king or Osiris?

Both Diodorus and Plutarch considered the sign of the eye to be the more important element. To their minds it implied that Osiris was the all-seeing eye, imparting his rays like the sun in the midst of night. Ruling in the shadowy realm of the dead, he was the Other – the complementary force of the solar eye reborn each day in the brilliance of dawn. The eye of the sun was the living image of the soul of Osiris (figure 4.3).

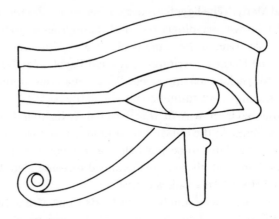

Figure 4.3   The eye of Horus – Osiris reborn, New Kingdom amulet, ca. 1300 BC. After Hornung, 158

Modern scholars have made various attempts to explain the etymology of the name Osiris, pronounced "wasir" in ancient Egyptian. Some have sought to explain the name by looking at the Egyptian sources, while others have ventured afield in search for linguistic and religious parallels.

The undeniable similarity of Osiris to the Mesopotamian Assar, the Good God, has been pointed out.[10] One of the designations of Osiris used from the Middle Kingdom on was Wennofer, the Good Being. Wennofer was frequently used as a personal name during the Old Kingdom and continued to be popular all the way until the Middle Ages in Europe in the form of Onofrio. Like the name of Osiris, the name of Assar was also written with the eye and the throne. Thus, the double identification of Isis with Ishtar and Osiris with Assar has been proposed, connecting the religious traditions of Mesopotamia and Egypt. From the Predynastic Period on, many ideas were shared between the two cultures. Some parallels such as the writing of the names of the Good God Assar and the Good Being Osiris may have been made deliberately after the development of writing.

In the *Golden Bough* Frazer pointed out the similarity of Osiris to other Near Eastern heroes, such as the Sumerian Dummuzi (Semitic Tammuz) and Adon, the Lord of Byblos. Both Tammuz and Adon were consorts of the great goddess Ishtar or Astarte. Both were sacrificed to affect the forces of fertility. The Greeks preserved the legend of Adon of Byblos in the popular story of Venus and Adonis.

Scholars who have sought the origin of the name of Osiris in Egypt have found the closest parallels in the Berber word *wsr*, meaning "the old one," and the Egyptian *wsr*, "the mighty one" (both languages were written only with consonants). These words were descriptive designations, like the names of the other gods, and may even have been related in meaning.

The unbreakable link between Osiris and Isis, as well as the sacrifice of Osiris, were indeed reminiscent of other Near Eastern myths on the same subject. The Nile flood, however, its coming and going heralded by the stars of Sirius and Orion, was without parallel. The complex nature of Osiris also seems to be peculiar to Egypt. All the references to Osiris in the Pyramid Texts indicate that he was a dead god. What was unique to Egyptian thought when compared with other Near Eastern religions was the idea of rebirth through Osiris that emerged between the lines. It was not Osiris himself who was made immortal or woke up to new life; new life was reborn from the mystical essence of the god. Only by becoming one with Osiris after death, by accepting the crux of his nature, were "the gates of heaven toward the horizon" flung open before the wandering soul. His force worked from the nether regions, hidden in the darkness that always sent up new life to the world. Osiris was "the one within," "the father and mother of people – they live from your breath and eat of the flesh of your body." In the words of Ramesses IV, his nature was more mysterious than that of all the other gods. The idea of sacrifice, of healing the rift to make life whole, was part of the story from the very beginning.

So was its connection to the rising of the Nile. From time immemorial the most important event in the lives of the people was the flood. Life depended on it. Charms and divinations were practiced on the night the river began to rise as late as the nineteenth century. Edward Lane, who published *Manners and Customs of the Modern Egyptians* in 1834, described how the people spent all night on the banks of the river, "some in houses of their friends, others in the open air," awaiting the first news about the rising of the river. The results were proclaimed by public criers in every district with the words: "God has been propitious to the lands! The day of good news!" A New Kingdom inscription at Silsila described how Ramesses II on the first day of the inundation threw into the Nile a written order commanding the river to do its duty.

The rising of the Nile was also associated with sacrifice, moreover human sacrifice. Lane describes the festival of cutting a canal that took place in Cairo shortly after the beginning of the inundation in 1834. The canal was opened near Rhoda Island, not far from the Nilometer. On this occasion a boat sailed from the port of Bulaq to the island,

> painted in a gaudy but rude manner ... with numerous lamps attached to the ropes, forming various devices, such as a large star ... It has also over the cabin a large kind of close awning, composed of pieces of silk and other stuffs,

35

and adorned with two pennants. It is vulgarly believed that this boat represents a magnificent vessel in which the Egyptians used, before the conquest of their country by the Arabs, to convey the virgin whom it is said they threw into the Nile.

Lane also quotes the Arab historian Makrizi and his account of the local customs encountered by the Arabs when they conquered Egypt, led by Amr Ibn el-As.

This historian relates that in the year of the conquest of Egypt by the Arabs ... Amr was told that the Egyptians were accustomed at the period when the Nile began to rise to deck a young virgin in gay apparel, and throw her into the river as a sacrifice to obtain a plentiful inundation. This barbarous custom, it is said, he abolished, and the Nile in consequence did not rise in the least degree during the space of nearly three months after the usual period of the commencement of its increase. The people were greatly alarmed, thinking that a famine would certainly ensue. Amr therefore wrote to the caliph to inform him of what he had done, and of the calamity with which Egypt was in consequence threatened. Omar returned a brief answer, expressing his approbation of Amr's conduct, and desiring him, upon the receipt of the letter, to throw a note which it enclosed into the Nile. The purport of this note was as follows: *From Abd-Allah Omar, Prince of the Faithful, to the Nile of Egypt. If thy flow of thine own accord, flow not; but if it be God, the One, the Mighty, to make thee flow, we implore God, the One, the Mighty, to make thee flow.* Amr did as he was commanded; and the Nile, we are told, rose 16 cubits in the following night.[11]

The association of the Nile with brides continues to this day. Before the inundation of the Nile was halted by the Assuan High Dam some forty years ago it was still customary in Cairo to make a corn doll called el 'arusa – "the bride" – for the festival of the inundation. As the waters rose, the doll was thrown in the river to the joyful cheering of the assembled crowds. In Sudan young brides wash in the Nile after their marriage ceremony for they believe that the river will bless them with children.

While the rising of the Nile was a festive occasion, celebrated as a symbolic wedding ceremony between the Nile and his bride as late as the twentieth century, the falling of the Nile was a time of mourning. Herodotus mentioned the Festival of Lights, the custom of lighting up all houses in Egypt on the night in autumn when the flood ended in commemoration of Osiris who was about to be buried.[12] Frazer thought that this celebration represented to the Egyptians a festival of All Souls.

The Festival of Lights lived on until late Roman times. In the fourth century AD, every year in Rome the procession of Isis went searching for the body of Osiris by torchlight, followed by a train of devotees carrying candles. The celebration, called Lychnapsia in the calendar of Philocalus, anticipated the Candlemass Day of Catholicism.[13]

By contrast, the spring equinox – the time of harvest – was a festive occasion. It was then that Osiris engendered a son. Merry processions marked this event by carrying an image of the god that had a triple male member.[14] Isis discovered she was pregnant when Hapi arrived in the summer and her tears turned to joy.[15] Their child was born at the winter solstice with the sun. For the rural communities along the river who had no access to the Pyramid Texts, the myth of Osiris was a guide to the seasons, the rhyme and reason of the Egyptian world. The god who fed his people with his own broken body and who always returned in the coming harvest naturally ruled supreme in their affections. While the other gods were worshiped only in their own districts, Osiris, Isis, and their savior-child were adored everywhere.

Divine kingship, the power that had bound the two lands together, may have been the principal contributor to the dissolution of the Old Kingdom. The monarchy had reached the height of its autocratic power in the Third and Fourth Dynasties. As the state atrophied during the Fifth, the power of the provincial rulers grew. Local rulers had become independent princes ruling their domains with little concern for central authority or, one suspects, for their subjects. The latter had no recourse to the king and his justice. New classes of people had emerged: priests, scribes, architects, and craftsmen who demanded recognition and reward. One may even speculate that further down the line similar pressures for advancement began to affect other segments of the population. All of these elements were wholly alien to the social structure of the kingdom created by the Thinite rulers. The age of absolutism waned. The diminishing of the royal authority and the king's decline from the status of absolute divinity probably allowed for numerous influences to germinate. The economic and social changes on every level were so profound that the upheavals continued for some two centuries.

The end of the Old Kingdom and the dissolution of the old order prompted changes in the concept of the afterlife. With the death of the king as god, people were suddenly cut off from their direct access to the divine. The gods of Egypt, temporarily united under the aegis of the divine king, went their separate ways back to their places of origin. Freed from religious fetters to the king and his guarantee to take all of society with him, individuals became responsible for their own rebirth. On the good side, everyone was allowed to aspire to an afterlife. Once the popular creed took over, Osiris became overwhelmingly popular while Ra, the exclusive god of kings, retired once more behind the walls of the temple at Heliopolis.

CHAPTER 5

THE MYSTERIES

Some time during the First Intermediate Period (2160–2055 BC) Osiris acquired the status of being the great judge of the dead in the next world, who died in autumn and came back to life after three days. During the Middle Kingdom (2055–1650 BC), his rites of resurrection came to be celebrated every year at Abydos in a public passion play that was to last for more than a thousand years.

The First Intermediate Period was a term coined to describe the aftermath of the breakdown of the Old Kingdom in Memphis that ushered in political and social turmoil. In the absence of any central authority, power had reverted to the local districts. A provincial family from Heracleopolis had seized Memphis, but their rule was recognized only in the north. The southern provinces were ruled from Thebes. In the wars that followed, battles were waged over the control of Thinis and the sacred valley of Abydos. Theban princes made incursions to the north, but their advance was halted by the monarchs of Assyut.

The country was disunited and parochial rivalry became the order of the day. In self-laudatory inscriptions local rulers boasted that they fed their own towns while the rest of the country was starving. The great proliferation of weapons included among the grave goods of ordinary people testifies to the overall insecurity of the times. Even administrators represented themselves grasping weapons instead of official regalia.

King Mentuhotep had reigned quietly over his Theban kingdom for fourteen years before hostility flared up again. With strong ties to the south, the Thebans had at their disposal seasoned Nubian soldiers. They were mobilized to lend combat strength in the battle that was to come. After amassing his forces, Mentuhotep marched north and took hold of Assyut. Mentuhotep II (2055–2002 BC), the founder of the Eleventh Dynasty, reunited the kingdom.

For ages to come the Egyptians commemorated Mentuhotep's valiant achievement. As late as the Twentieth Dynasty numerous private inscriptions praised his name. The resurgence of all forms of art in the later years of his reign suggests that he was successful in restoring peace. Building on a monumental scale was revived with the construction of a funerary temple at Deir el Bahri on the west bank of Thebes. It combined elements of Upper Egyptian architecture with pyramid tombs, achieving striking innovations.

This inspiring symbol of the reunification of Egypt marked a new beginning. It was the first royal structure to overtly stress Osirian beliefs that had overwhelmed Egyptian religion. Mentuhotep celebrated the Heb Sed festival at the temple. During the ceremony the king's statue with the flesh painted black, grasping the crook and flail of Osiris, was buried in a pit under the temple. The figure's black flesh evoked the black earth of Egypt, the act of burial – the sacrifice of Osiris. The rite symbolized more than just royal rejuvenation; it endowed the temple and the kingdom with perpetual renewal and eternal life. This statue was discovered by chance when in 1900 the horse of the inspector of the Egyptian Antiquities Service (Howard Carter) stumbled, its front hooves having fallen into the subterranean access passage. Mentuhotep's black statue is now in the Egyptian Museum in Cairo.

Although it had such a promising start the Eleventh Dynasty collapsed only nineteen years after Mentuhotep's death. The king was succeeded by his son Mentuhotep III (2004–1992 BC), an energetic organizer and builder of monuments. The art of relief was restored to its former glory and the tradition of the Memphite School revived. An expedition was dispatched to the land of Punt, the precise location of which still remains a matter of dispute. It has variously been identified as the coast of Somalia, southern Sudan, or the Eritrean region of Ethiopia, where the indigenous plants and animals relate most closely to those depicted in the Egyptian reliefs and paintings.

Mentuhotep III was succeeded by Mentuhotep IV (1992–1985 BC). He may have been a usurper, since he was omitted from the king lists. The Egyptians described his reign as "the seven empty years." The only noted event of his reign was sending a quarrying expedition to the Wadi Hammamat. Amenemhat, the vizier who led the expedition, recorded two remarkable omens the party had witnessed. The first, a gazelle giving birth to her calf on the stone chosen for the king's sarcophagus. The second, a sudden rainstorm in the harsh desert terrain that revealed a large well full of water to the brim. These two miraculous events predicted the rise of a new royal family. Amenemhat (1985–1956 BC), favored by the gods, became the founder of the Twelfth Dynasty.

The most significant move of the new king was to establish a new capital in the Fayoum oasis, some 50 kilometers southwest of Memphis. The Fayoum, the closest oasis to the Nile valley, had a natural lake that watered a vast expanse of palm groves. The kings of the Twelfth Dynasty joined the lake to the Nile by a web of canals and waterways, converting it into a large reservoir of water.

The patron god of the Fayoum was the crocodile Sobek, who possessed numerous sanctuaries on the lake's shores. Herodotus described how a real crocodile was selected and "taught to be tame and tractable . . . They adorn his ears with ear-rings of molten stone [colored glass] or gold, and put bracelets on his fore-paws, giving him daily a set portion of bread; and after having thus treated him with the greatest possible attention while alive, they embalm him when he dies and bury him in a sacred repository."[1] People who met their deaths from crocodiles were treated with the same respect as those who had drowned in the Nile. The law compelled the inhabitants of the city where the body was found to bury it in a sacred precinct with all possible magnificence. "No one may touch the corpse, not even any of the friends or relatives, but only the priests of the Nile, who prepare it for burial with their own hands – regarding it as something more than a mere body of a man – and themselves lay it in the tomb."[2]

The choice of the out-of-the-way oasis as home for the royal court was a bold move. It suggests a violent beginning for the new ruling family, compelled to establish its own power base at a new location. Being closer to the Delta may have played a part, as the Delta border had become besieged by tribes from Asia Minor. The capital was called Amenemhat Ity Tawy – "Amenemhat, the seizer of the two lands" – and its exact location remains undiscovered.

Amenemhat strengthened the control of the frontier in the eastern Delta by building massive fortifications called Walls of the Ruler. Other fortresses in the eastern Delta and in Nubia protected Egypt's borders. The king's military expedition to Nubia marked the beginning of a steadfast colonial policy toward Egypt's southern neighbor.

The country of Nubia had always played a part in Egypt's history. Nubia, literally "land of gold," was said to begin at the first cataract at Assuan and end at the confluence of the White and the Blue Niles, more than 1,500 kilometers upstream at Khartoum. Before the building of the Assuan High Dam and the creation of the 500-kilometer Lake Nasser, the area below the first cataract at Assuan marked the beginning of a different landscape. Edward Lane gives the following description of the terrain, quoting the Arab historian Makrizi:

> This district is narrow and very mountainous, extending but little from the Nile. Its villages are far apart, one from the other, on each bank. Its trees are the date

> palm and the mookl (dom palm) . . . The fields are not naturally irrigated by the
> Nile: being too elevated; the inhabitants sow by the feddan (about an acre and
> one tenth) . . . and employ cows to raise the water from the river by means of
> wheels. Wheat is scarce among them, barley is more plentiful and soolt (a kind
> of barley). They cultivate and sow the land a second time [every year]; on
> account of its being so confined. In the summer after having manured it with
> dung and earth, they sow dukhn (a small kind of millet), dura (millet), ja'wur
> (another kind of millet), sim'sim (sesame) and lubiya (kidney-beans).[3]

Egyptians and Nubians were connected by the same river and shared
the same fate brought on by the flood. The people of Nubia were made up of
numerous tribes, many of them nomadic, but the Fellahin of the Nile valley
shared a common way of life with the Egyptians and worshiped many Egyptian
gods. Competition for the control of goods traveling up and down the Nile had
always played a part in the relationship between north and south. From early
on, Egypt had tried to capitalize on its access to the Near East and the Mediterranean. Most sensitive of all was the area of Wadi Allaki in northeastern
Nubia, with its gold mines. The control of this region was a cause of ceaseless
contention.

Amenemhat's colonial policy toward Nubia marked the beginning of Egypt's
firm grip on Nubian resources. His son Senusret I (1956–1911 BC) proclaimed
Lower Nubia to be a province of Egypt. Senusret's successor Amenemhat II
(1911–1877 BC) personally led a military campaign to Nubia; the area was
raided for captives to serve in Egypt's army. Amenemhat had also discovered
a new source of forced labor in Asia Minor. His campaign to Palestine boasted
to have brought back 1,554 Asiatic captives.

By the time of Senusret II (1877–1870 BC) peace and prosperity had settled
in. There were no military campaigns; the greatest achievement of the time
was the inauguration of the Fayoum irrigation project that extended the
amount of farming land in the oasis. Dykes and canals were constructed to
regulate the flow of Nile waters into the Fayoum lake, Birket Haroun, and its
surface was greatly enlarged. Herodotus described the lake, called Moeris by
the Greeks, as a great marvel:

> The measure of its circumference is 60 schoenes, or 3,600 furlongs, which is
> equal to the entire length of Egypt along the sea coast. The lake stretches in
> its longest direction from north to south, and in its deepest part is of the depth of
> 50 fathoms. It is manifestly an artificial excavation, for nearly in the centre,
> there stand two pyramids, rising to the height of 50 fathoms above the surface
> of the water . . . The water of the lake does not come out of the ground, which
> is here excessively dry, but is introduced by a canal from the Nile. The current
> sets for six months into the lake from the river, and for the next six months into

> the river from the lake. While it runs outward it returns a talent of silver daily to
> the royal treasury from the fish that are taken, but when the current is the other
> way the return sinks to one-third of that sum.[4]

Senusret II was succeeded by Senusret III (1870–1831 BC). The latter was the most "visible" of the Middle Kingdom rulers.[5] His legend gathered momentum over time, giving inspiration for the famous figure of Sesostris described by both Manetho and Herodotus. The main domestic achievement of Senusret III was to strip the provinces of their power by abolishing the office of district ruler once and for all.

The king campaigned in Nubia in years six, eight, ten and sixteen. These wars appear to have been very brutal, with the Nubian men killed, their women and children enslaved, their fields burnt, and their wells poisoned. Stelae were set up at the fortresses of Semna and Uronarti near the second cataract, forbidding Nubians to travel north of the border. The texts included a double "blessing and curse" for succeeding kings who would maintain the border and those who might fail to do so. There was at least one campaign against Palestine. Egyptian troops reached as far as Shechem in Samaria and still more Asiatics were forced to make their way to Egypt. In addition to being captured as prisoners, some may have been bought as slaves, as the biblical story of Joseph indicates (Genesis 37: 28–36).

Senusret's son Amenemhat III (1831–1786 BC) had a long and peaceful reign usually regarded as the cultural peak of the Middle Kingdom. He prudently maintained and safeguarded the achievements of his predecessors. He had the privilege of undertaking numerous building projects that culminated in the construction of the Labyrinth, as his funerary temple was known to posterity. This building does not exist any longer; all we have is Herodotus' awe-struck account of it, written during his visit to the Fayoum:

> I visited this place, and found it to surpass description; for if all the walls and
> other great works of the Greeks could be put in one, they would not equal, for
> labor or expense, this Labyrinth . . . The pyramids likewise surpass description,
> but the Labyrinth surpasses the pyramids. It has twelve courts, all of them roofed,
> with gates exactly opposite one another, six looking to the north and six to the
> south. A single wall surrounds the entire building. Half [of its] chambers [are]
> under ground, half above ground; their whole number . . . is three thousand.
> The upper chambers I myself passed through and saw and what I say con-
> cerning them is my own observation; of the underground chambers I can only
> speak from report: for the keepers of the building could not be got to show them,
> since they contained (as they said) the sepulchers of the kings who built the
> Labyrinth and also those of the sacred crocodiles. Thus, it is from hearsay only
> that I can speak of the lower chambers. The upper chambers, however, I saw

with mine own eyes, and found them to excel all other human productions; for the passages through the houses, and the varied windings of the paths across the courts excited in me infinite admiration, as I passed from courts into chambers, and from the chambers into colonnades, and from the colonnades into fresh houses, and again from these into courts unseen before. The roof was throughout of stone like the walls; and the walls were carved all over with figures; every court was surrounded by a colonnade, which was built of white stones, exquisitely fitted together. At the corner of the Labyrinth stands a pyramid, 40 fathoms high, with large figures engraved on it, which is entered by a subterranean passage.[6]

The numerous subterranean chambers of the Labyrinth were probably a recreation of the netherworld of Osiris, with its obscure passages and hidden abodes. In texts from this period, the perilous journey through the netherworld dominated the literary imagery. References to the Mysteries of Osiris evoked secret rituals reserved for the initiated.

The Mysteries of Osiris may have been influenced by the ancient religion of Thoth – his cult center at Hermopolis was situated in the same district as Abydos. Mystery had always been the attribute of the god of magic. The cult of Thoth championed its own creation myth. On the Island of Flame four elements had come into being at the same time. Together with their unnamed creator they were the Great Five. The Pyramid Texts said that "the Waters spoke to Infinity, Nothingness, Nowhere, and Darkness" and creation began. The four became eight – male and female. Out of the union of the eight came the primeval egg and out of the egg came the light of the sun.

During the Middle Kingdom, Thoth's magic was invoked to help on the journey to the netherworld. The legend about the Book of Thoth, one of the most enduring stories about the god, was connected to the netherworld. It was said in a Ptolemaic papyrus:

Thoth wrote the book with his own hand and in it was all the magic in the world. If you read the first page, you will enchant the sky, the earth, the abyss, the mountain, and the sea: you will understand the language of birds in the air, and you will know what the creeping things in the earth are saying, and you will see the fishes from the darkest depths of the sea. And if you read the other page, even though you are dead and in the world of ghosts, you could come back to the earth in the form you once had. And besides this, you will see the sun shining in the sky with the full moon and the stars, and you will behold the great shapes of the gods.

Throughout Egyptian history, various heroes had been searching for the Book of Thoth. In the Ptolemaic papyrus it was prince Neferkaptah who found the golden casket containing the scroll at the bottom of the Nile at Koptos. He wrote down the magical words of the book, washed the ink off with beer, and then drank the beer and Thoth's wisdom with it.

The development of the Fayoum Oasis was the last achievement of the Twelfth Dynasty. Six generations of vigorous and capable rulers had consolidated the kingdom, restored Egypt's domains, and created new opportunities. With the death of Amenemhat III the creative powers of this family ran dry. Amenemhat IV (1786–1777 BC), seemingly a colorless personality, left the throne to his sister queen Sobek-Neferu (1777–1773 BC). Several headless statues remain of her, one of them sporting the Osirian "Heb Sed" cloak. It would appear that Sobek-Neferu performed the ritual hitherto reserved for kings. The queen used feminine titles, but several masculine ones were employed on occasion. With this first woman on the pharaonic throne the dynasty that had elevated Egypt to new heights came to an end. The tombs of Amenemhat IV and queen Sobek-Neferu have not been found.

The rulers of the Thirteenth Dynasty, founded by Wegaf some time around 1759 BC, continued to use Ity-Tawy as their capital. Egypt still controlled the area of the Second Cataract in Nubia, Nile floods were measured, the same bureaucratic system was maintained, and royal monuments continued to be built. The dynasty, however, was made up of different families and the reigns of these kings were short-lived. It is still not clear how long they ruled and how the question of the succession was resolved. Most of these kings were no more than names to us written on king lists; the names were generally combined with that of Sobek, the crocodile god of the Fayoum.

The modest burial of king Awibra Hor, a mere shaft tomb dug within the funerary complex of Amenemhat III, reveals the impoverished circumstances of the new dynasty. During the rule of Sobekhotep I the Nubians revolted and the area slipped out of Egyptian control to be ruled by a line of native kings at Kerma. In the northeastern Delta, the Egyptians maintained their position of power somewhat longer. By the later years of the dynasty, however, they pulled back from this region as well.

In the first half of the seventeenth century BC movements of people in Western Asia, triggered by migrations of Indo-Aryans, affected Egypt. Walls of the Ruler, the chain of fortifications built by Amenemhat I, were penetrated and there was a steady infiltration of nomadic tribes. Their numbers were swelled by the presence of numerous Asiatic slaves, freedmen, and laborers. A papyrus in the Brooklyn Museum mentions that a single Theban household possessed up to ninety-five Asiatic slaves.

A few people from this west Semitic stratum of the population had succeeded in ascending to the office of kingship in Dynasty Thirteen, probably due to their military capability, among them Khendjer – "boar" – who had two mud-brick pyramids built for himself at Dahshur and Saqqara. The capstone of one of Khendjer's pyramids, now in the Cairo Museum, has the image of the reborn Osiris at the top. By associating himself with Osiris and the rising sun, Khendjer hoped to arise to immortality.

Shortly after the reign of Sobekhotep IV (ca. 1725 BC), the unity of the kingdom began to break up. By the end of the dynasty, the conquered Asiatics had become the conquerors. With their superior battlefield tactics, using horses (hitherto unknown in Egypt), they encountered little trouble in establishing themselves at Avaris in the eastern Delta. The Egyptians called them Hekau Khasut, rulers of foreign (literally, mountainous) countries, a name used to designate Bedouin chieftains. The Greeks pronounced these words as Hyksos and described them as shepherd-kings. When these nomadic horsemen swept across the land, the kingdom fell apart once again.

During the Middle Kingdom a sense of renewal was felt in every sphere of life. Profound social transformations that marked the end of the Old Kingdom had inspired fresh efforts to reinvent the world of Egypt. As the new epoch merged with the old, the movement pushed forward, fueled by the torrent of creative energy, the growing cultivation of individuality among the learned, and by the development of distinctive literary styles. Middle Kingdom literature became Egypt's classical age. The Tale of Sinuhe, Eloquent Peasant, and Shipwrecked Sailor introduced new themes and literary forms. The scribe Khety, who composed Instructions of King Amenemhat for Senusret I, also wrote the Satire of the Trades, a humorous work describing the duties and rewards of the scribal profession.[7] In it, a father tells his son: "A scribe is the task-master of everyone . . . I shall make you love books more than your mother." This composition enjoyed wide circulation and became one of the standard texts read in scribal schools. Dialogue Between a Man Tired of Life and his Soul (Ba) was the earliest treatise on the subject of suicide. The art of rhetoric developed, verses sung to the accompaniment of a harp grew into complex poetic compositions, and religious hymns abounded, eventually inspiring the biblical psalms.

The age introduced greater humanity in writing, remarkable realism in portraiture, and "democratization" of religious practices. A genuine leveling of traditional customs had revolutionized Egyptian society. Sacred writings, quoted from the Pyramid Texts and elaborated upon, decorated the wooden coffins of ordinary people. Their prolific number ceased only after the introduction of the mummiform coffin in mid-Twelfth Dynasty, which was less well suited to long inscriptions because of its irregular human shape.

The Book of Two Ways, described as "the earliest hermetic work in Egypt,"[8] was written out on coffins from Deir el Bersha, the necropolis of the city of Thoth. It was a guide to the netherworld, with detailed maps drawn on coffin floors. The netherworld had seven gates and "a fiery court" around the sun. The desired destination was Rosetau at the "boundary to the sky" wherein lay the body of Osiris. One spell described it as "locked in darkness and surrounded by fire." It was said that whoever gazed on the body of Osiris could not die.

All those who wanted to spend eternity in the vicinity of Osiris's sacred kingdom dedicated autobiographical stelae at Abydos. Some five hundred stelae, now in the Egyptian Museum in Cairo, contain the same words:

> Oh, you, who live upon earth and who pass by this stone, you who love life and hate death, you priests of all ranks [followed by a list of priestly ranks], you will pass on your blessings to your children if you say: "An offering given by the king and by Osiris, Foremost of the Westerners, may they give a million bread, beer, meats, clothes, incense, perfumes, and the sweet north breeze, all the good and pure things created by heaven, born by the earth, brought forth by the Nile, by which god lives, to the soul of NN [the individual name added], justified in Ma'at."

By the early Thirteenth Dynasty a royal decree of Wegaf (also inscribed by Neferhotep I) had to be issued to prevent people from setting up more stelae within the precinct of the temple. The punishment was the burning of the remains – eternal damnation.

The new outlook on the world had changed the religion of Osiris. His character was experienced anew at a time when all faith in traditional values was lost. Already in the Old Kingdom the Egyptians believed in a posthumous court of judgment, presided by an unidentified great god who was like the great king in the earthly court. When the kingdom collapsed and justice ceased to be practiced on earth, redemption before the heavenly tribunal became all the more important. As royal tombs were being looted and ordinary people remained unburied, conventional ideas about material provisions were no longer sufficient. Did eternal life really depend only on the ritual burial and the bestowal of offerings? Was a privileged position in life a guarantee for anything in the next world?

For answers, people turned to Osiris. He was the voice that spoke to every heart, the undisputed sovereign of the dead whom everyone had to encounter when the hour had struck. As a god who shared human suffering and death, Osiris would know the human heart and understand the trials and tribulations of earthly life. One could even argue that at the time of crisis, during the First Intermediate Period, he took the place of the king as a unifying force in the community, offering faith and moral values as guiding principles in society. Union with Osiris became a promise of eternal life that extended far beyond all safeguards guaranteed by the ever-repeated funerary cult. Belief in such a union was heartfelt, profound, and virtuous.

Middle Kingdom pharaohs acknowledged Osiris's supreme position. By the time Egypt was reunified by Mentuhotep II, Osiris had become the patron god of all the cities of the dead. The site of Abydos and its temple was generously endowed by Senusret III and Sobekhotep III. Neferhotep I recorded on a stele that he went to Abydos as a pilgrim to take part in the Mysteries of Osiris.

The Mysteries focused on the judgment of the soul after death. The otherworldly court had become a supreme, scrutinizing tribunal and anyone who wanted to share eternal life under the aegis of Osiris was subject to its decisions. Texts from the Book of the Dead, known from papyri of the New Kingdom, described the judgment in great detail. Although these are records of a later date, they probably referred to Middle Kingdom originals. By the time the Book of the Dead came to be widely circulated in the New Kingdom, it was "packaged" for mass consumption and sold on demand. The content was predetermined, only the space for the individual name was left empty to be filled by the person who bought the copy. Everyone could simply affix his or her name between the designations: "Osiris" and "Justified in Ma'at." These ready-made sacred books were then dedicated in the tomb of the deceased, who now had magical writings at their disposal to guide them through the netherworld.

To gain admittance to the judgment hall, or as the Egyptians called it, "the hall of twin truths," the dead had to undergo a trial. It took the form of a cross-examination:

"Who are you?" say they to me,
"What is your name?" say they to me.
"I am the lower root of the papyrus plant,
'he in the olive tree' is my name." [designations of Osiris]
"Where have you gone past?" say they to me.
"I have gone past the place to the north of the thicket . . ."
"What has been given you?"
"A flaming fire and a faience column." [the amulet of Osiris]
"What have you done with them?"
"I buried them on the shores of the Ma'ati waters during evening sacrifice.
I lamented over them,
took them up,
extinguished the fire,
broke the column
and threw it into the pool . . ."

The questions and answers were then followed by a final summons: "Come then and step through this gate of twin truths, for you know us!"

In the judgment hall, Osiris sat enthroned surrounded by forty-two judges (this number evokes the forty-two district rulers of Egypt). A pair of scales was placed before him to weigh the heart of the deceased against a feather, the symbol of Ma'at. The keeper of the balance was Thoth, the god of magic. Anubis, the guide of souls, led the deceased before Osiris. Nearby, a monster called the "devourer" stood ready to swallow those who were condemned. Thoth asked four questions of the deceased:

"Why have you come?"
"To be announced."
"What is your condition?"
"I am free of every sin."
"To whom shall I announce you?"
"To him, whose ceiling is fire, whose walls are living serpents, whose house-floor is the flood."
"Who is that?"
"Osiris."
"Then take yourself there: behold, you are announced!"

Faced with the prospect of eternal damnation, the deceased now had to recite "the negative confession" before all the judges, a full statement of forty-two offenses, faults, and sins that he had *not* committed. The confession was meant to set the morality of the deceased in a favorable light. It revealed, if not the moral practices, at least the moral ideals of society. The deceased solemnly protested that he had not oppressed his fellow men, made anyone weep, and committed neither murder nor adultery. He had not born false witness, upset the balance of Ma'at, nor taken milk from the mouths of babes. He had given bread to the hungry, water to the thirsty, and clothes to the naked. If judged righteous, he was admitted to the divine sphere of existence – the epithets "Osiris" and "Justified in Ma'at" were affixed before and after the personal name. In a final act of acceptance it was declared:

"A truly righteous one.
Let him be given bread and beer,
that issue from Osiris.
He shall live forever among the followers of Horus."

Osiris did not judge the dead, he only presided over their judgment. People's hearts were weighed on the measuring scales against the feather of Ma'at; if found wanting, the souls were excluded from future happiness. Only thus were gods capable of influencing destiny. The wicked were punished not because Osiris rejected them, but because they were wicked. Everyone's conscience was his own judge.

All justified souls were admitted to the community of gods and spirits, modeled after the pattern of earthly society. The giving of the bread and beer that issue from Osiris was not unlike the Christian bread and wine offered at the mass of the Eucharist. Osiris, the Good Being, gave sustenance to the righteous and pointed the way to immortality with the shepherd's crook.

The arrangement of the text into a dialogue suggests that it was originally recited, probably with the assistance of a priest. The "Instructions for Use" attached to the text quoted above recommended that

> a man says this speech when he is pure, clean, dressed in fine clothes, shod in white sandals, painted with eye-paint, anointed with the finest oil of myrrh . . . He for whom this scroll is recited will prosper and his children will prosper. He will be the friend of the king and his courtiers. He will receive bread, beer, and a big chunk of meat from the altar of the great god. He will not be held back at any gate of the Western Land . . . He will be a follower of Osiris. Effective a million times.[9]

The same moral ideals were asserted on the stelae set up in the cemetery of Abydos. A man professed the following in his epitaph:

> I gave bread to the hungry and clothes to the naked and ferried across in my own boat him who could not cross the water. I was a father to the orphan, a husband to the widow, a shelter from the wind to them that were cold. I am one who spoke good and told good. I earned my subsistence in Ma'at.

It remains an open question how far the term "mystery" applies to the rites performed at Abydos. Mystical initiation in Egypt was widely documented by the Greeks. Herodotus mentioned being initiated in the mysteries of a god whose name he refused to disclose during a nocturnal passion play. Plutarch confirmed that the Mysteries of Osiris involved secret initiation: "Osiris is common to all, as the initiates know."[10] Scholars would argue, however, that it was the result of the Greek influence on Egypt, rather than the other way around. A regrettable lack of contemporary written records that would shed some light on the subject presents a problem. However, the oath-bound secrecy of mystical rites would have precluded the possibility of written records and it becomes a circular argument.

In the ancient Egyptian language, mystery was designated by the word *hes* – "to usher in, enter." This verb described the investiture of pharaoh, the installation of a priest in office, and initiation into the secrets of Osiris. The word *seshta*, with the meaning of making secret and inaccessible, had a similar meaning to the Greek *mysterion*. From this word was compounded the title Master of Secrets, written with the Anubis jackal. Mystery was present in the underworld because that was where divine life rose from death.

Within stone-built temples secret rites always took place in secluded precincts. A single shaft of light from the roof usually lit the innermost room or the holy of holies in every temple. The semi-darkness emphasized the mystical aspect of the cult performed within. There were rooms in the temple of Philae on the portals of which it was written: "Nobody is *ever* allowed to enter." Plutarch described Egyptian temples as "partly consisting of open and airy corridors and colonnades, partly [of] dark, subterranean rooms which have a likeness to caves and graves."[11] Entering these chambers would have evoked a journey to the netherworld. "Do not reveal what you have seen in the Mysteries of the temple," commanded an inscription at Dendera. To do so would take away the power of initiation.

It is particularly difficult to understand the nature of the secret ceremony of the resurrection of Osiris. We know that in Roman times it was celebrated by a select group of priests in rooms where none of the uninitiated were allowed to enter. According to the third century AD Christian writer Hippolytus, the ceremony had a sexual basis: "The Egyptians have the Mysteries of Isis, holy and august and not to be talked about with the uninitiated. But these Mysteries are simply the lost *pudenda* of Osiris for which she of the seven stoles and black robe goes in search."[12]

Mysteries were wordless sermons. The silence of initiation was meant to imply the profoundest revelation of the truth that was all embracing and the source of all teaching. Mysteries led to a knowledge that was neither necessary nor possible to clothe in words. The seeking and finding of Osiris probably held deepest secrets for the initiates – we do not know how he was found, even the identity of what was found. The act or the object – if it existed – would have had a transparent meaning to the celebrants. It would have been contained in the very fact of the Mysteries being celebrated and experienced at all, self-evident once people had adopted the common standpoint of the wordlessly initiated. Mysteries were kept silent. Proclaimed, they would have been but words; kept silent, they were *being* pure and simple. "Happy is he who has seen such things," Euripides wrote, describing the Mysteries of Demeter at Eleusis that culminated with the finding of a stalk of grain: "His lot after death will be different from that of all the others." In this sense, miracles and epiphanies probably were witnessed in Abydos.

When the worship of Osiris emerged as the principal religion during the Middle Kingdom, the mystical aspects of his worship probably took on their essential forms as well. Some may have been practiced from the very beginning. While we can only speculate about the secret rites preformed in private, in public, the resurgence of religious feeling was expressed with great fervor in the annual reenactment of the Passion of Osiris. It was a public celebration rather than a hidden mystery.

Pilgrims from all walks of life came to Abydos for the occasion. Visitors were offered accommodation and food, magical papyri, lanterns, statuettes, and amulets to be dedicated at the holy sites. Vestments and flowers were laid in the ancient cemetery. Osiris's tomb in Abydos (originally the tomb of Djer) came to be known as Hemhemet – "great in fame." The festival took place from the twenty-third to the thirtieth of the month of Khoiak (November).[13]

An inscription from the Coffin Texts reads: "I have come, that I might behold Osiris, that I might live by his side, that I might rot by his side." Abydos became to the Egyptians what Jerusalem is to Christians and Mecca to Muslims. Every year, pilgrims from all over Egypt would gather to seek and find the body of Osiris. It was a drama out of doors, a collective celebration of the god's resurrection.

At the appointed hour, the funerary barge of Osiris set sail from Thinis to Abydos, followed by an array of small boats. The voyage hearkened back to the ancient burial of the Thinite kings. Pilgrims crowded the riverbanks, hailing the god as he crossed the river on his annual journey to the Western Land. The barge moored at Abydos, ministers brought forth the sacred ark, and the crowds shouted: "Osiris has been found!" Guided by a priest in a jackal mask and others who impersonated the protagonists of the legend, the cortege made its way to the ancient royal cemetery. All those who had a tomb, statue, or stele put up near the processional road hoped to participate for all eternity.

On the way, the foes of Osiris, led by Seth, attacked the mourners. They were duly repelled; charms and incantations were sung to dispel evil powers and hostile spirits. The trial of Horus and Seth before the tribunal of the gods was enacted. Seth was condemned and banished. At last, the procession arrived at the tomb of Osiris. Reading, chanting, and prayers for the god's resurrection were spoken at the vigil by the tomb. Then, priests entered the sepulcher by the western door and reverently laid the chest of Osiris on a bed of sand in the chamber. There they left him to his rest and departed by the eastern door.

The chest buried in the tomb contained the earth body of Osiris. Plutarch described how every year earth and silt from the inundation were placed in a wooden chest and planted with seeds to symbolize the body of Osiris.[14] After the chest was buried the death of the god was mourned for three days and nights.[15] During this time it was customary to bury figurines of Osiris, made of earth, corn, and vegetable paste, in the ground. Three images were made, symbolizing his dead, re-membered, and risen body. They possessed sacramental, magical power.

The resurrection was preceded by "the night of sleeping." During that night, the "Sem Priest" – the son of Osiris – slept on a low couch in front of the god's statue in the Golden House – the temple sanctuary. He called upon the soul of his father, hovering in the night air: "Come to me, descend to me!"[16] In his dream, he encountered the soul, caught it like a bird, and instilled it in the statue. In the morning he announced that the buried god had come back to life.

The festival culminated with the celebration of the resurrection. The pillar of Osiris – the ancient symbol of the harvesters – was erected in the temple court to the jubilant rejoicing of the assembled crowds and the living image of the resurrected one brought out on a portable boat and displayed. The Egyptian phrase for a religious festival was "god's appearance." Merriment and dancing concluded the weeklong gathering.

Ikernofret, an official at the court of Senusret III, wrote the earliest account of the festival. The king had appointed him to organize the Mysteries, endowing him with the titles of Master of Secrets and Son of Osiris. He described how he made the god's barge and statue:

> I acted as the beloved son of the Foremost of the Westerners. I furnished his great bark, the eternal, everlasting one . . . I decked the breast of the lord of Abydos with lapis lazuli and turquoise, fine gold and all costly stones, which are the ornaments of a god's body. I clothed the god with his regalia in my rank of Master of Secrets . . . I was pure of hand in decking the god, a priest whose fingers are clean.[17]

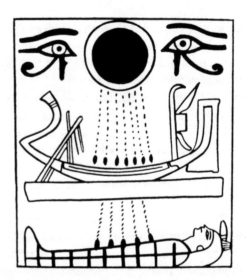

Figure 5.1   The boat of Osiris, Dynasty 21 funerary papyrus, ca. 1050 BC. After Hornung, 121

The theme of the Mysteries was the eternal coming of life from death (figure 5.6). Once established, the festival lived on for thousands of years, lasting as late as Roman times. Plutarch explained:

> It is not therefore without reason that they relate in their myth that the soul of Osiris is eternal and indestructible, but that his body is frequently dismembered and destroyed by Typhon (Seth), whereupon Isis in her wanderings searches for it and puts it together again. For what *is* and *is* spiritually intelligible and *is* good prevails over destruction and change.[18]

CHAPTER 6

RISE OF THE EMPIRE

In the New Kingdom (1550–1069 BC) the cult of Osiris developed in unprecedented ways. This period ushered in a religious innovation: monotheism. For the first time in history the idea was expressed that there was only one god. Monotheism changed religion forever. In the aftermath of the monotheistic revolution, the myth of Osiris merged with the religion of Ra, and Osiris became an enlightened savior-god. Once again, history shaped the fate of the myth.

The evolution of religion at this time can be understood only by looking at the dramatic historical events that led to the founding of the Egyptian empire. Foiled national pride and the particular disposition of the new royal family that was to rise at Thebes played a part in the curious development religion was to take. The war of liberation against the Hyksos encouraged the rise of larger than life personalities. Patriotic feelings went hand in hand with the growing mistrust of "Asiatics."

At the end of the Middle Kingdom, the Hyksos had conquered the Nile delta by storm. Riding high and mighty upon their horses, they seized the land

> by main force . . . easily, without striking a blow . . . Having overpowered the rulers of the land, they burned their cities ruthlessly, razed to the ground the temples of the gods . . . Finally, they appointed as king one of their number whose name was Salitis. He had his seat at Memphis, levying tribute from Upper and Lower Egypt and always leaving garrisons behind in the most advantageous positions.[1]

Having devastated the weakened Egyptian kingdom, the shepherd-kings established themselves as rulers of the land. Chaos and destruction followed in their wake. Generations later, queen Hatshepsut still talked about "their roving hordes . . . overthrowing what had been made . . . The temple of the lady of Cusae . . . fallen into dissolution, the earth had swallowed up its noble sanctuary and children danced upon its roof." They stopped at the town of Cusae, opposite Hermopolis in Middle Egypt. Thereafter, they returned to Avaris in the eastern Delta, which became their preferred seat of residence.

Originally, Avaris (modern Tell el Daba) was a camp in the Walls of the Ruler, the defense complex built in the Middle Kingdom to prevent Asiatics from entering the country. Positioned on the caravan route that connected north Sinai with the Levantine coast, within a few generations Avaris had grown into a busy trading outpost. A steady influx of new settlers from Lebanon and Cyprus had swelled its population. By the time the Hyksos chose it as their capital, it had become a major Levantine colony. The list of commodities traded at Avaris included "chariots and horses, ships, timber, gold, lapis lazuli, silver, turquoise, bronze, axes without number, oil, incense, fat, and honey."[2]

The Hyksos ruled Egypt from Avaris and Memphis for some hundred and fifty years. Their exact origin is still unclear, but evidence suggests that they were not a single, ethnically congruous group, but, rather, a culturally related alliance of tribes of different ethnic origin that had come from Syria. They were listed by Manetho as Dynasty Fifteen.[3] They worshiped Seth. The enemy of Osiris may have been chosen as their patron because of his similarities to the Syrian storm god Ba'al.

But the foreign conquerors, like many who were to follow, were rapidly becoming Egyptianized. The new elite seemed to prefer marrying local women. When faced with running Egypt, they had no choice but to hire Egyptian administrators and reopen the scribal schools. Even kings went to the trouble of learning the Egyptian script. It was said that the Hyksos king Apepi was "a scribe of Ra, taught by Thoth himself . . . [blessed] with numerous deeds on the day when he reads faithfully all the difficult passages in the writings, as flows the Nile." Egypt could not be ruled without help from educated Egyptians. Even the army garrisons came to employ Egyptian commanders.

The shepherd-kings, however, seem to have remained content with mastering the script mainly for the purpose of collecting tax. They closed down the royal workshops, since they had no use for them. Usurpation of earlier monuments was considered more practical. When a ruler wanted a statue of himself, he simply chose one he liked, had the old names chiseled out and added his own.

The southern boundary of the Hyksos remained at Cusae. Contemporary texts mentioned the imposition of taxes on all Nile traffic north of Cusae. Even more lucrative was the control of the trade route through the oases of the western desert to Nubia. It provided the king of Avaris with access to Nubian gold. The kings of Kush at Kerma, the traditional enemies of Egypt, seized the opportunity to strike an alliance with the foreign invaders and reap the rewards of the gold trade.

It was over Nubia that strife began to brew. At Thebes, a line of local kings had continued to rule independently of the Hyksos. They were cut off from any contacts with the Delta and had to make do. Their impoverished circumstances can be seen in all the traces they left behind. Their monuments consisted mainly of stelae, commemorating valiant efforts to keep their kingdom alive.

Neferhotep fought the Hyksos, but they retaliated, destroying some of the temple of Karnak. In such uncertain times the king's role as military leader became increasingly pronounced. Rahotep claimed to have restored the temples at Abydos and Koptos, while an inscription of Sobekemsaf II records sending a military expedition of 130 men to the Wadi Hammamat. The inscription was written in a clumsy mixture of the hieroglyphic and hieratic scripts, betraying the unfortunate loss of traditional skills.

The funerary monuments of these kings, listed as Dynasties Sixteen and Seventeen by Manetho, were also modest. The precise dates of their rule remain uncertain. They were buried in simple wooden coffins decorated with a feather pattern that conveyed the image of the soul's flight to heaven.

Whatever they lacked in material resources the kings of Thebes made up for in their proud spirit. Their faith in the ancient tradition was unbending. The blockade of Thebes and the control of the cataract region by the kings of Kush became intolerable. Having mastered the horse and the new war tactics, the Thebans set out to liberate Egypt.

King Sekenenra Ta'a led his regiments against the foreign invaders and died in battle from a fatal blow to his head, still visible on his mummified body.[4] Kamose "the Brave," probably his son, continued the struggle. It was essential for the Thebans to conquer Kush before proceeding against the Hyksos. By the third year of Kamose's rule, Nubia was again under Egyptian control. Kamose decided to march against Avaris. It was ruled by Apepi, the most powerful of all the Hyksos kings.

Kamose sent Nubian scouts to spy out the position of the enemy garrisons. Then he dispatched his battle fleet and led his army on foot. North of Cusae the army intercepted a messenger from Apepi to the king of Kush. Kamose realized that he had to send his men to Bahareya Oasis to cut Apepi's lines of communication with the Kushites. At Avaris he deployed his fleet to blockade the city, patrolling the banks to prevent a counter-attack. As his soldiers despoiled the area, the palace women looked out at the Egyptians "like lizards within their holes." But Apepi refused to engage him and Kamose did not attack. Instead, he returned to Thebes only with plunder.

There was no immediate follow up by the Thebans as both Kamose and Apepi had died in the aftermath of the campaign. At Thebes Kamose was succeeded by the boy Ahmose (1550–1525 BC), probably his younger brother.

In the interim, the queen mother Ah-hotep ruled as regent. At Avaris, Kamudi succeeded Apepi.

It took eleven years for Ahmose to follow in Kamose's footsteps. Ceaseless preparation for war probably marked his early reign. At last, there was a lucky turn of events. The Indo-Germanic Hittites had made powerful thrusts from Anatolia against Syria. Finally, they succeeded in conquering Aleppo, effectively cutting off the Hyksos from their allies. Ahmose used this window of opportunity and decided to attack Memphis. His plan was to cut off the retreat of the Hyksos across northern Sinai to Palestine.

Ahmose had to wait for three months for the Nile inundation to subside in order to move his men and chariots across the valley. At last, his fleet besieged Avaris and he led his army into attack. There were several battle engagements and the siege was maintained. In the end, giving up the siege in despair, the king of Avaris concluded a treaty by which the Hyksos were obliged to depart from Egypt. Evidence from Avaris confirms the picture of a mass exodus after Ahmose's victory.

At last, the foreign invaders were driven out and Ahmose could have easily uttered the words, later used by the boastful queen Hatshepsut: "I have banished the abomination of the gods and the earth has removed their footprints." For Ahmose, the expulsion of the Hyksos was only the first step in reunifying the kingdom. In order to consolidate his victory over the shepherd-kings he led his army in pursuit all the way to Palestine. His aim may have been to destroy the remnants of the Hyksos and possibly to exploit the vacuum left behind, in order to expand Egyptian dominions.

The reunification of Egypt took place only during the last years of Ahmose's twenty-five year rule. At last, Ahmose enlisted the power of Osiris. To legalize the new dynasty, he built a funerary monument at Abydos in the form of a pyramid, relating himself to the ancient ancestor cult. This gesture was aimed at ensuring continuity with the great kings of the past. The last royal pyramid ever built, it came to be venerated as an oracle in the Ramesside Period.

At the end of all the wars, little time was left for Ahmose to rule. The soldier-king died, having accomplished the dream of a long line of kings: he had defeated the foreign invaders, reunified Egypt, and paved the way for the rise of the greatest empire in Egypt's history – the New Kingdom.

Ahmose was succeeded by his son Amenhotep I (1525–1504 BC), possibly, like his father, still a minor at his accession. The queen mother Ahmose-Nefertari figured prominently during his entire reign, as well as during the reign of his successor, Thutmose I. The rise of the new ruling family, the Eighteenth Dynasty, was marked by the strict royal custom of brother marrying sister. Amenhotep's mother Ahmose-Nefertari was Ahmose's sister. This lady enjoyed every royal title in existence: "great royal sister, wife, and mother," as well as "god's wife of Amun" in her role as priestess. Together with her son, she was venerated as the patron of the Theban Necropolis and was often represented with black or blue flesh, the colors of the resurrection.

The king's greatest interest lay in the sphere of culture. At his court he had succeeded in assembling a creative elite the likes of which had not been seen since the Middle Kingdom. Theologians, poets, architects, artists, and scientists gathered around him. Papyrus Ebers, a medical discourse dated to year nine of the king's reign, recorded the solar rising of Sirius, providing a solid basis for the chronology of the New Kingdom. The astronomer Amenemhat invented the first water clock. The architect Ineni created a new kind of royal tomb; it was rock cut and hidden in the Theban cliffs, reflecting the obscure paths of Osiris's underworld.

Religious thinkers were encouraged to invent original concepts and write entirely new compositions. The earliest preserved copy of the Book of the Hidden Chamber, later known by its abbreviated name of *Amduat* (The Book of What is Netherworld) was written at this time. It described the sun's voyage through the hours of the night – the kingdom of Osiris. At night, the whole of the mythology was let loose. Sailing on the otherworldly Nile, Ra passed through regions of "blackest darkness" and "barren, sandy deserts, wherein lived monster serpents." A host of otherworldly demons inhabited the netherworld: spitting snakes with human heads sprouting from their coils, hawk-headed crocodiles, star-men, child-gods, and keepers of time and the hours. The Being of Light encountered the blessed dead plowing fields of corn and the damned burning in lakes of fire. At times, even the infernal river vanished from view and Ra and his company were forced to tow the boat through virtually impenetrable rock, not unlike the Nile cataracts. In the next hour, in another kingdom, Ra boarded the boat and sailed towards the Gate of Dawn. Antedating Dante by three thousand years, the *Amduat* was the earliest description of the Egyptian heaven and hell.

Hymns to the rising and setting sun were composed, using new imagery and poetic idioms. At court, scribes began writing enigmatic or "cryptographic" spells, developing a mysterious script in which obscure meaning underlay well-known hieroglyphs, making the script comprehensible only to the initiated. The latter seem to have taken delight in the texts' ambiguity and exclusiveness at the time when the first alphabetic writing systems were being developed in the Levant. The alphabetic scripts were easier to master and literacy became more widespread.

It had become fashionable to speak foreign languages and numerous Semitic loanwords entered the Egyptian vocabulary. For burials of ordinary people, Books of the Dead were supplied in readily available collections on papyrus. Belief in magic and its varied practices continued to thrive; along with the new royal funerary texts lived the age-old folk tradition.

At Abydos, Amenhotep completed the pyramid complex begun by his father, but as a builder he focused on Karnak. Amun, the patron of Thebes, had become the icon of the new ruling family. His temple was enlarged to become a veritable labyrinth of pylons, courtyards, and chambers. Egypt had once again entered a glorious age.

Amun's career had begun as the local god of a small village, probably a variation of Min, the god of Koptos. By the Twelfth Dynasty the followers of Amun had gained political ascendancy over their neighbors and made their god the chief of all the area. In the New Kingdom Amun had assimilated the attributes of Ra and began to rule the nation as Amun-Ra, king of the gods. He formed the triad of Thebes with his consort Mout and their son Khonsu. According to Papyrus Harris I, written in the reign of Ramses III, the inventory of Amun's temple listed "5,000 divine statues, more than 81,000 slaves, vassals, and servants, well over 421,000 head of cattle, 433 gardens and orchards, 691,334 acres of land, 83 ships, 46 building yards, and 65 cities and towns."

As a composite divinity, however, Amun did not have a unique theology, only duties to protect the king and the newly founded Egyptian empire. The name of his consort, Mout, meant simply "mother." Their child Knohsu was a moon-god who had assumed many of Thoth's attributes. The statues of Khonsu had the reputation of casting out evil spirits, but one gets the impression that their main use was to obtain a steady flow of offerings to the attendants of the temple at Karnak.

Not one of these gods had any particular story attached to them, other than protecting members of the royal family in one way or another. Amun was said to have fathered Hatshepsut and his oracular power was used to reinstate Thutmose III. As the power of Thebes grew, the High Priest of Amun came to rule supreme over the other priesthood.

Amenhotep ruled for twenty years, leaving no offspring. The succession seems to have passed with ease to Thutmose I (1504–1492 BC), although he was not a royal son. Thutmose probably married into the royal family by marrying queen Ahmose. It was with her that Thutmose fathered the future queen Hatshepsut. He also fathered Thutmose II with a non-royal wife, Mutnofret. During his reign "god's wife of Amun" Ahmose-Nefertari died and was replaced by Hatshepsut.

Thutmose I reigned for eleven years. His relatively short rule was in inverse proportion to the impact he had on the Eighteenth Dynasty. In the first two years he led a campaign to Nubia, delivering the final deathblow to the kings of Kush and incorporating Kush into the Egyptian empire as a province. Egypt now stretched over 2,000 kilometers from the Mediterranean to the fourth cataract in Sudan, by river.

The king had a flare for theatricals. On his return to Thebes, he stood on his ship in triumph, "all countries in his grasp, with the defeated Nubian bowman hanged head down at the [front] of the boat." Thutmose established military headquarters in Memphis, a more strategically suitable location for contacts with Asia Minor. From then on, every crown prince received military training in Memphis and commanded the Egyptian army. Egypt's foreign policy remained oriented towards Asia for centuries to come.

At this point, Thutmose had decided to claim divine descent. At the temple of Osiris in Abydos, having brought gifts of his own cult statues, he had himself proclaimed the son of Osiris. At Giza, he dedicated a stele with his names and titles, reviving the worship of the Great Sphinx as Horus of the Horizon. By this time, the colossal statue was a thousand-year old relic and Giza with its three pyramids had become a popular site. By marking his presence there, Thutmose had visibly linked himself with the deified kings of the past. All the subsequent rulers of the New Kingdom followed the custom of self-deification.

Thutmose I was followed by Thutmose II (1492–uncertain BC). The rule of the latter is usually described as "ephemeral." Having had the misfortune of marrying his half-sister Hatshepsut, Thutmose II disappeared from history sometime between years one and three of his reign. He may have been the father of Hatshepsut's daughter Neferu-Ra. He also fathered a boy, Thutmose, with a non-royal wife, Isis. Upon the king's untimely death, the boy Thutmose III officially became king, but his aunt and stepmother acted as regent.

It has been argued that Hatshepsut (1479–1458 BC), the daughter of queen Ahmose, saw herself as the legitimate heir of Thutmose I.[5] Every step she took demonstrated that she had learned a great deal from her father. From the very beginning, she was preparing her own daughter to take over in similar fashion.

The ambitious new regent enforced her position by adopting a traditionally male coronation name, "Ma'at-ka-ra." Moreover, she began to transform herself into a king in all her public appearances. Statues and reliefs represented her with male attire, beard tied to her chin, bare-chested and sporting the pharaonic kilt with a lion tail. On her monuments she described herself as divinely engendered by Amun and officially proclaimed heir by Thutmose I. She had been selected during a public appearance of Amun's statue by means of an oracle. Some texts even contained warnings: "He who shall do her homage shall live, he who shall speak evil in blasphemy of Her Majesty shall die." Her contemporaries seem to have been well aware of her demeanor and if they saw much of her rule as a scam, they did nothing about it. "Egypt worked for her, head bowed," the official Ineni wrote in his autobiography. Hatshepsut got away with it for twenty years.

It helped that there were no military threats from abroad during this time. Aside from local uprisings in Nubia that were swiftly dealt with, peace and prosperity reigned. An expedition to Punt was made more sensational by bringing back the queen of Punt in person to pay homage to the Egyptian monarch. The scene was immortalized on a relief that represented the portly foreign queen as part of the exotic goods paraded at Thebes.

As builder of monuments Hatshepsut far surpassed her predecessors. While making notable additions all over Egypt and Nubia, the queen-pharaoh particularly lavished her attention on Thebes. The temple of Karnak rose to unprecedented splendor. To emphasize the new dominant role of Amun the festival of the Beautiful Feast of the Valley was set up. Once a year, the statue of Amun of Karnak, carried in procession on a barge called Powerful of Prow, went to visit his harem and then made the rounds of the sacred places in Thebes. To this day in Thebes (modern Luxor), revelers carry boats on their shoulders every year during the celebration of the feast of Abu el Hagag, the Muslim saint. The boats are now related to the life-story of the saint who brought Islam to Luxor.

The capital became the microcosm of the Egyptian universe. A hill on the West Bank at Medinet Habu became venerated as the primeval hill of creation. The site received a temple to the Ogdoad, the eight primeval creator-gods who lay asleep until the end of time. Deir el Bahri, where Mentuhotep II had built his funerary temple, received a magnificent addition. Although based on its Middle Kingdom predecessor, the queen's temple outsized it to such a degree that it became barely visible in the shadow. Its pillars were embellished by colossal images of the queen as Osiris, complete with a curved beard attached to her chin.

Hatshepsut initiated the necropolis in the Valley of the Kings, building a tomb for herself and her father at the foot of a limestone rock with a pyramid-shaped peak, sacred to the goddess Meretseger – "she who loves silence." It was within its jagged cliffs that vast beehives of corridors and chambers were carved out for the dead pharaohs until the end of the New Kingdom. The remote desert valley hearkened back to the celebrated city of the dead at Abydos.

The western mountain of Thebes became the new residence of Osiris. In tomb decorations he was often represented rising out from the mountain's edge at dawn, his arms risen and his manhood ready to inseminate the new day. The queens (except for Hatshepsut who ruled as king) were buried several miles south in the hills of Hathor in what became the Valley of the Queens. Like Osiris, the heavenly cow was shown stepping out of the western mountain at daybreak.

Between the two sacred valleys court officials carved out their own entries to the netherworld. Inside the perpetual night of the tombs, the parched hills of western Thebes were transformed into a brightly colored land of plenty inhabited by the gods. Fresh pools of water flowed in lush palm groves, beautiful goddesses peered out of flowering trees offering fruits, vines ripened, and banquets were served. The bird-like souls of the dead fluttered to and fro, drinking from the waters of eternal life and keeping watch over the living.

It was during Hatshepsut's time that Osiris's enemy Seth became demonized once again. Associated with the hated Hyksos, he was banished into the desert along with his defeated followers. In New Kingdom tombs Seth was often represented as a pig. The Egyptians regarded the pig as an unclean animal and many abstained from eating pork. Herodotus observed: "if a man in passing accidentally touch a pig, he instantly hurries to the river and plunges in with all his clothes on."[6]

The queen's prolific building program may have benefited from her association with the architect Senmout, whose statues adorned her buildings. Although of humble origin, Senmout had risen to become "the greatest of the great ones in all the land." He was often shown with princess Neferu-ra in what was possibly a brazen allusion to royal statues of queens represented with male consorts. The role reversal was complete and unabashed. Affluence and material splendors required no excuses. A new time had come. Thebes ruled the world.

At some point after completing the queen's funerary temple, Senmout had begun making a tomb for himself at its footing. Although planned to have regal proportions, it was soon abandoned. Had Senmout fallen out of favor? Or had the boy Thutmose III grown up? It seems that the queen's young co-regent had become desperate at being robbed of kingship. It was later said that he had received a divine prophecy in the Karnak temple that he would become king in spite of her. He seems to have made it happen.

In the twentieth or twenty-first year of Hatshepsut's reign the kingship reverted to Thutmose III alone (1479–1425 BC). As soon as he took over, Thutmose III wasted little time in eliminating his co-regent from history. Hatshepsut disappeared entirely, her statues smashed to pieces, her images hacked out of reliefs, her obelisks walled in, and her names erased from every monument. Although the defacement of her monuments may not have occurred until a new co-regency was declared, the enmity harbored by the new king could hardly be concealed. She was omitted from the king lists. Her father Thutmose I was removed from the joint tomb and reburied in another. The queen's crypt was left unfinished and despoiled, the fate of her mummy unknown. Perhaps the greatest irony of all was that on relief representations Hatshepsut and Thutmose III can hardly be distinguished from each other, so similar were their faces with prominent aquiline noses. The only visible difference was the king's more virile chest with a heavier upper torso and broader shoulders.

While keeping many officials who served under Hatshepsut, Thutmose III set out to demonstrate his military prowess. Being thwarted by a woman for twenty years required that he prove himself a man. For seventeen years he campaigned in Syria, enlarging Egypt's dominions. When his wars of conquest were complete, Egypt's borders extended to the banks of the Euphrates. The Mittani kingdom, Egypt's powerful enemy, was forced into alliance, clinched by royal marriage with several Mittani princesses. Children of defeated Syrian rulers were sent to Egypt to be Egyptianized. The boys were brought up at the royal court, the girls found themselves in the royal harem.

In the field Thutmose III discovered the greatest reward of war: booty. He may even have continued to campaign intermittently until his forty-second regnal year just to obtain spoils from his rich neigbors. The prize taken after the siege of Megiddo included 894 chariots, among them two covered with gold, 200 suits of armor, including two made of bronze that belonged to the chiefs of Megiddo and Kadesh, as well as 2,000 horses and 25,000 head of cattle.

Syrian objects became the fashion of the day. Tombs of the new military elite were packed with Syrian goods. The Syrian deities Astarte and Reshef appeared among native gods. The capital began to assume a cosmopolitan air. A veritable river of gold flowed to Egypt from Nubia. The king showered the new riches on almost every temple in Egypt and Nubia. All over the Nile valley ancient shrines were arrayed to celebrate the proud accomplishments of the new empire. The king's buildings were monumental but graceful; their smooth, elegant proportions and clear-cut forms still create the impression of an age of new classicism in art. Judging by the artistic accomplishments, the age of Thutmose III represents the empire in its mature, self-confident aspect. At least part of this cultural ambiance was due to the king's steady, prudent rule in the latter years of his reign.

The temple of Amun at Karnak received the lion's share of the king's gracious building endowments. Reliefs in the newly built Akh-menu – "Effective of Monuments" – temple at Karnak depicted, among other things, exotic trees brought back and planted in the capital. A masterpiece of architecture, it was designed to celebrate the king's perpetual renewal in the afterlife as well as to maintain his cult for ages to come. On its walls the king was represented venerating his own kingship.

The colossal height of the king's obelisks has not been surpassed. Two of these towering granite needles, today in London and New York, were erected in front of the temple of Ra in Heliopolis. Two more soared high in the middle of open courts on the east–west axis of the Karnak temple, with the disk of the rising and setting sun creating a luminous halo around their sharp peaks. More than a thousand years later, the Roman emperors took yet another of Thutmose's obelisks to embellish Rome. It now stands in front of the Lateran church in the heart of Christendom.

Thutmose's accomplishments were scrupulously recorded in historical annals, establishing his reputation as a great warrior for more than a thousand years: "[he is] abler than a million men in a great army. No equal has been found [to him], a fighter assertive on the battlefield." A lively story circulated about his taking of Joppa (modern Jaffa). The king's general had put about the word that he was dead and that the tribute of two hundred baskets was being sent to the city as an offer of peace. Then the Egyptian soldiers hid in the baskets; once brought inside the city, they escaped and let the army in. The Egyptian story precedes the legend of the Trojan horse by several centuries.

Thutmose III had numerous wives. In the fifty-first year of his rule he took his son Amenhotep (with the priestess Meryt-ra) as co-regent and shared rule with him for a little more than two years. It is possible that the monuments of Hatshepsut were altered at this time in order to prevent any descendants of her family line from claiming the throne. Some of her buildings were obscured by new additions. The memory of the queen had been steadily and systematically erased by her once co-regent. Thutmose's deliberate choice of foreign and non-royal women may have been inspired by being all too aware of the dangers posed by the powerful women in the family whose rank and wealth surpassed those of men.

The king seems to have instilled this disposition in his son and successor Amenhotep II (1427–1400 BC). Throughout his reign the official consort of this king was his mother Meryt-ra. Numerous women had borne him children, but none of them assumed the title of queen. No son was named co-regent. In fact, the complete lack of attention paid by Amenhotep II to his women and children eventually caused deadly infighting for the throne.

Like his father, Amenhotep II cultivated his manly image. As a youth he had lived in Memphis and trained horses in his father's stables. Renowned for his athleticism, he had himself portrayed on a relief shooting arrows through copper targets while driving a chariot with the reigns tied around his waist, almost as a forerunner of Achilles. His legendary reputation was carried on even in his tomb, where he was buried with a mighty bow designed to shoot enormous arrows.

Also like his father, Amenhotep II led two campaigns to Syria. Unlike his father, however, Amenhotep II seems to have been driven by his brutish nature. Seven defeated chiefs from the area called Takshy were taken back to Thebes upside down on the royal barge and six of them hung from Amun's temple wall. The seventh was carried all the way to Napata in Kush where his body was exhibited as an example to the local people. Plunder from the first campaign comprised 6,800 deben of gold and 500,000 deben of copper, a staggering amount, along with 550 captives, 210 horses, and 300 chariots.

The king's successor, Thutmose IV (1400–1390 BC), had received no recognition of any kind by his father. His mother Ti'a had not been mentioned on any inscriptions, except later, after her son's accession to the throne. Following the custom established by Thutmose I, crown princes received military training in Memphis. Young Thutmose was sent to Memphis, but he was one of many. Amenhotep II had failed to select anyone as crown prince and his male heirs fought fiercely for dominance.

Thutmose IV commemorated his rise to the throne on a stele he placed between the forepaws of the Great Sphinx at Giza. It described a prophetic dream that had come to him when he fell asleep in the shadow of the Sphinx's huge smiling face:

> Look at me, observe me, my son Thutmose," said the Sphinx. "I am your father Horus of the Horizon, Khepri-Ra-Atum. I shall give you kingship [upon the land before the living] . . . [Behold, my condition is like one in illness], all [my limbs are ruined]. The sand of the desert, upon which I used to stand, [now] confounds me; and it is because I want to make you do what is in my heart that I have waited!

Thutmose cleared the Sphinx from the invading sands and the mighty god made him king.

The idea of legitimizing the seizure of power by divine oracles had already been invented by Amenemhat I in the Twelfth Dynasty and reused by Hatshepsut and Thutmose III. This oracle, however, involved a different god and the king went one step further than his predecessors. Not content with being merely the son of the sun, Thutmose IV became the living incarnation of the sun. The elevation of the sun-god to supreme status as well as the king's own identification with him set a precedent that would lead to unexpected consequences. The idea of the sun-king was to change both kingship and religion.

After Thutmose IV's accession, the names and images of his brothers were defaced in their father's Giza temple, in yet another act of *damnatio memoriae*, by now commonplace in the family. The destruction of names and images was believed to magically destroy the people represented.

If Thutmose IV's disposition appeared somewhat extravagant, that of his son Amenhotep III (1390–1352 BC) eclipsed it by far. Having ascended the throne as a boy, he seems to have been under the strong influence of his mother Mutemwiya. He was deified early in the reign and identified with all the national gods of Egypt. At an early age he married Tiye, the young daughter of an official from Akhmim. The marriage was celebrated with great pomp and ceremony in the capital, where newly made statues of the royal couple were worshiped as divine. Tiye's powerful presence continued to loom throughout the king's thirty-eight year rule. They had four daughters and two sons. The elder Thutmose was installed as Sem Priest in Memphis.

Amenhotep III differed considerably from his predecessors. He had no interest in war. After going through the motions of organizing a traditional Nubian campaign that by now followed every accession, he gave up all war-like pretenses and spent the rest of his life in the sumptuousness of his court, scarcely to emerge again. He never set foot in the Asian provinces. Dynastic alliances and diplomatic marriages took the place of conquest. Gifts from Egypt's gold surplus bought years of peace.

His was the age of international relations. Diplomatic letters were exchanged with the kings of Mittani, Arzawa, and Babylon. Royal marriages sealed long-established alliances. Gilukhepa, the daughter of the Mittani king, was sent along with 317 ladies in waiting to the king's harem. Then followed the marriage with the Babylonian princess. When a new king ascended the throne of the Mittani, Amenhotep III dutifully married his daughter as well. Emissaries and gifts were sent to the rulers Mycenae, Phaestos, and Knossos. The king's court was cosmopolitan, secularized and splendor loving. While ordinary people worshiped the portly king as a god of plenty, the affluence of the elite had reached its zenith. Thebes reveled in her wealth.

Amenhotep III's main activity was building. Egypt's capital was transformed to become Homer's "Thebes of a hundred gates." His predilection for dramatic architecture was most visible in the funerary temple built on the west bank. It was of enormous size and furnished with colossal statues of both well-known and obscure Egyptian gods, many represented with human bodies and animal heads. Unfortunately, the huge building was systematically plundered by the Ramesside kings, having become a veritable quarry for sculpture, relief, and stone within a few generations.

The only remnants that still stand are two seated statues of Amenhotep III with queen Tiye at their feet that once guarded the first gate. Too large to be moved, they still tower over the plain and can be seen from any point on the west bank. They have been a well-known destination for pilgrims since antiquity. The Greeks wrote that the northern sculpture emitted a melodious sound at dawn, like the snapping of a harp-string, as soon as the morning sun fell upon it. At the setting of the sun and during the night it uttered very lugubrious sounds. The Greeks believed that the statue represented Memnon, the son of Dawn, nephew of Priam and king of the Ethiopians, who behaved with great courage at Troy and was killed in combat by Achilles. Memnon welcomed, they wrote, the first smile of his beautiful mother and bemoaned her absence during the gloomy watches of the night. This extraordinary phenomenon was witnessed by some of the most exalted and illustrious men of the Greek world who inscribed their names on the pedestal of the statue to attest that they had heard the sound. Among them was the geographer Strabo, who was ingenious enough to acknowledge his inability to determine whether the voice proceeded from the head of the statue, or from its base, or even from some of the people who were crowding around it to listen to the wonder. Cambyses, king of Persia, wreaked his vengeance on the statue by causing it to be broken and thrown upon the ground. But its wonderful power of speech still remained and the superstition of the people was more firmly riveted to it than ever. Finally, the Romans mended the statue, but the sound disappeared after their restoration. To this day Amenhotep's sculptures are called the colossi of Memnon.

The king's palace was also built on the west bank, south of the funerary temple. Standing on the shores of a vast artificial lake connected to the Nile by a canal, it was approached through a great harbor that sheltered several pleasure boats. Gardens, courtyards, and separate lodgings for the king's court surrounded the royal quarters. Houses of attendants, servant dwellings, artisan workshops, and markets huddled outside the palace walls. Villas of nobles and courtiers clustered around them. The royal residence was an entire city. The Egyptians called it "the dazzling sun disc." The king who lived within it was the living image of the sun.

In spite of the worldly splendor of his court, Amenhotep III cultivated lively religious interests. In fact, he seems to have been pious to the point of superstition. He revived many forgotten animal cults and built colossal statues of animal gods, among them 600 granite images of the lion-headed goddess Sakhmet, believed to have healing powers. Was he trying to placate her? The Mittani king Tushratta, his son-in-law, wrote in a letter that he sent a statue of the goddess Ishtar to help cure the ailing Egyptian king.

Amenhotep III delegated the tasks of running the empire to a number of capable officials, endowing them with titles and wealth. Since the lingua franca of diplomatic correspondence was Akkadian, scribes were expected to be bilingual. His favorite was Amenhotep, son of Hapu, a scribe from the Delta promoted to royal architect. This brilliant man of humble origins had close contacts with the royal family and in his old age held the title of steward to princess Sitamun. He directed the erection of the colossi of Memnon and on a statue of himself set up at Karnak he wrote: "I was introduced to the Book of the God, I saw the transfigurations of Thoth and was equipped with their Mysteries." Amenhotep, son of Hapu, may be the first documented Hermetist.

He was granted the privilege of having a funerary temple of his own, not far from the king's. In time, the little temple of the architect became a place of veneration that attracted pilgrims for thousands of years. Like his predecessor Imhotep, Amenhotep lived on in popular memory as a sage. By the Late Period, he was worshiped as a god of healing. It is after his name that the site became known as Medinet Habu.

The king's last years seem to have been clouded by illness that could not be exorcised. He celebrated three consecutive "Heb Seds" of Osirian rejuvenation in the hope of repairing his failing health. He died in the summer of 1352 BC and was buried in a secluded valley that branches off from the Valley of the Kings.

As the elder son Thutmose had predeceased his father, the vacated throne passed to the younger Amenhotep. The son of sun-king ascended the throne as Amenhotep IV (1352–1336 BC). The Eighteenth Dynasty had abounded in eccentrics. Every king and queen in the family had been made in his or her own mold. Conquest and sudden enrichment might have encouraged inflated personalities. However, even by the outlandish standards of the time, the new king was a phenomenon. His like had never been seen before.

CHAPTER 7

GOLDEN PHARAOHS

The new pharaoh introduced monotheism to the history of religion. It had such a profound effect on religious thought that it became impossible to return to the old ways without attempting a reformation. Religious doctrines developed during this reformation reinvigorated Egyptian religion and gave impetus to ideas that later flourished in Greco-Roman Egypt and eventually influenced the rise of Christianity.

In 1352 BC, when he ascended the throne of Egypt, Amenhotep IV was already a man with a vision. Somewhere in the open courts of his father's palace he had a revelation. God had spoken to him. He had shown himself as One, mother and father, creator of all. Amenhotep was transformed. The path had been chosen for him. He wrote poetry, inspired by the voice he heard:

> Splendid you rise, O, living Aton, eternal lord,
> you are radiant, beauteous, mighty,
> your love is great, immense.
> Your rays light up all faces,
> your bright hue gives life to hearts,
> when you fill the Two Lands with your love.
> August god who fashioned himself,
> who made every land, created what is in it,
> all people, herds, and flocks,
> all trees that grow from the soil.
> They live when you dawn for them,
> you are the mother and father of all you made . . .
> You are one, yet a million lives are in you.[1]

The god was Aton and he was his messenger. In Egyptian tradition, Aton was the sun disk, one of the aspects of the sun-god. Yet, to the new king, this particular manifestation had become more important than any other.

Becoming a king only strengthened his conviction that god's word should be revealed to all. Driven by the vision of a pure, unexploited religion, he set out to reform the spiritual and temporal estates.

In year four he sent the High Priest of Amun into the desert, delegating him the task of running a quarrying expedition. In the High Priest's absence, he built a temple to Aton that boldly stated his new beliefs. Aton was the sun-disk whose life-giving rays streamed down on all creation. He was deathless and eternal and everywhere present; nothing could come to pass without his will. Rich and poor were equal in his sight; if one received him, one became his servant, for his being was love. He was the only god, all others were idols. The king who dwelled in truth was his representative on earth, both mother and father to his people.

Amenhotep's colossal statues were made after his own instructions: they flaunted his gaunt face, slanted, faraway-looking eyes, spindly neck, sagging torso with a pot belly, female pudenda, rounded, feminine thighs, and thin legs. Just as strange was his face – a queerly long face with prominent cheekbones and the secret, ironical smile of a dreamer hovering about the thick lips (plate 4).

In Amun's temple, stone pharaohs stood on either side of gates, majestic, godlike giants. Here, this swollen, lanky human stared down from forty pillars, a man who saw further than other men. The whole of his stone-imprisoned form was instilled and tense with fanaticism. This is how the fourth Amenhotep saw himself. His wife Nefertiti and their eldest daughter were his sole companions on the temple walls. This royal family with strange, exaggerated features that verged on caricature had replaced divine triads. Monotheism was the new tenet in religion, naturalism the new style in art.

For the clergy, who had become comfortable under the lavish rule of his father, this was open war. Pharaoh had done the unthinkable: he had flouted Amun, the ruler of the universe. Aton, his disembodied, abstract deity had little immediate appeal. Furthermore, temple and state had been so entwined for thousands of years that their separation might create inconceivable chaos. In defying organized religion pharaoh had broken the dam of religious discipline. By his reasoning, everyone could be his own priest. This could not be allowed to last. The priesthood of Amun had to retaliate swiftly and firmly. They had to confront this royal insurrection.

However, pharaoh had no interest in ruling quietly; his path lay elsewhere and he was after something much bigger. He wanted to reform the relationship between man and god. For the priesthood, this was heresy. Pharaoh had overstepped his boundary. For pharaoh, in the face of Theban opposition, there was only one thing left to do. Taking his family and immediate retinue, Amenhotep IV embarked on the royal barge and sailed away.

Half-way up to Memphis a wide valley on the east bank of the Nile appeared as the new Eden, a landscape untouched by human hands. Gentle hills sloped down to a distant skyline where the sun rose in glory. Seen from aboard the ship, the outlines seemed to move and shimmer. This would be the new royal capital, Aton's Horizon (Tell el Amarna). In it, the king would rule to please his creator. In year five a new city was built on virgin soil, "belonging to no god or goddess." Boundary stelae were set up to mark its domains and the king vowed never again to set foot beyond them. He changed his name to Akhenaton, "the enlightened spirit of Aton," and looked after the children of god.

The founding of the new city brought division into the royal family, for the queen mother refused to follow her son into the wilderness. Thebes was her city and the Golden House of pharaoh her palace. The king's sisters also stayed at Thebes.

Once settled, Akhenaton set out to eradicate all traces of the past. Gangs of iconoclasts swarmed through the land as far as Soleb in Nubia. Every time they encountered the name of Amun, including personal names and tips of obelisks, they took out their chisels and carved it away. Amun had to disappear. Even the tomb of his father Amenhotep III was desecrated and the name of Amun removed from his personal name.

Other gods were targeted as well, especially those with animal forms. Osiris was proscribed, darkness and death denied. With Osiris the split in religious thought became an open gulf: on the one side was the god of light and on the other the god of darkness. They were mutually incompatible, like day and night, life and death. There was no answer to what happens after death, no discussion between Aton and Osiris, except for the verse:

> When thou [Aton] goes down in the western horizon,
> the earth is in darkness, as if it were dead.

Tombs moved from the west side to the east, to face the rising sun. Temples were closed down and cults forbidden. Religious festivals came to an end. The wrath of the king was unsparing; there was to be no god but Aton.

In the new capital he ushered in a new age. Palm trees waved proudly along its streets, pomegranates reddened in the gardens, and in fish pools floated rosy lotus flowers. People drove about on light carriages driven by horses adorned with ostrich plumes. Houses were of wood, airy and fragile like pavilions, their reed columns light and brightly colored. On the walls, paintings of flowers and sycamore trees swayed in the eternal spring. Ducks with brilliant wings rose in flight from papyrus thickets. A general looseness of form and liveliness of movement had entered Egyptian art. In writing, the vernacular language superseded the formal rhetoric of old.

At the heart of the city stood the temple, open to the sky, without any shadows. Even the lintels above doorways were open in the middle. The king worshipped his god in open courtyards studded with many small altars for offerings. No cult image was needed, as god was there for all to see. No talismans, protective eyes, or strips of papyrus inscribed with magic texts were sold in the temple. Aton required neither magic, nor gifts, nor sacrifices, but came freely to everyone who believed in him.

The king's family lived in two palaces, one for receiving foreign envoys, the other with a "window of appearances" from which they greeted their subjects and distributed golden necklaces to the favored. The only decorations in art were pictures of the royal family. They displayed an intimacy never before seen in Egyptian art, let alone among royalty. The king, his wife, and children kissed and embraced under the rays of god whose love pervaded all creation.

Pharaoh's courtiers described themselves as orphans who owed their existence to him. In their private houses they kept small altars and shrines with images of the royal family that replaced the ancient household gods. Personal piety became identical with loyalty to pharaoh. His work was likened to the inundation of the Nile that sustained people and all living things. Not even in death did pharaoh intend to leave Aton's Horizon. After his city was built, he sent workmen to the eastern hills to hew out eternal resting places for himself, his family, and courtiers.

In year twelve, Akhenaton had dispatched a small military expedition to Nubia. But this was to remain his only show of force. The same year a great ceremony took place at Aton's Horizon. All foreign countries were gathered together as one, to pay tribute to the Egyptian king. He received them informally, surrounded by his family and wearing simple day robes. He gave them images of Aton and made plans to build temples in their distant lands.

Content as he was in Aton's Horizon, he still felt the tug of duty. Nefertiti had given him six daughters. The question of succession may have urged him to marry another wife, Kiya, possibly the mother of the boy Tutankhaton. The king's son-in-law Smenkara was made co-regent. In a city of their own, court and family lived protected from the fury of the clergy and the pressures of the empire. Aton's Horizon had shut itself away within the dreams and visions of pharaoh, unconcerned with the outside world.

Outside the city, division cut through every level of Egyptian society. With the temples shut down, hundreds of priests, scribes, and temple attendants had to look for other means of livelihood. Many were forced to toil the fields. The position of the army was diminished as pharaoh had no interest in war, but the able general Horemhab kept resentment in hand. The army enforced pharaoh's orders and all insurrection was cut down. The people of Egypt, prevented from practicing their age-old customs, probably grieved for their beloved faith. Perhaps the dismal truth was that the new religion turned out to be at least as bigoted as the old.

The affairs of state required attention. The few city-states that had remained loyal to Egypt cried for help. But their pleas went unheard. While Amenhotep III had lent a personal touch to his correspondence with foreign dignitaries, his son left foreign affairs to his officials. Letters were addressed to his mother Tiye, who still remained a figure of authority. But pharaoh simply wouldn't budge. Things were beginning to get out of hand.

Unrest and rebellion probably followed, though we have no record of it. The mighty priesthood of Amun probably plotted their revenge and return. Pharaoh's officials probably demanded that the army engage in Syria, that the clergy and the people be placated, that a firm hand rule the empire. Thebes probably seethed with discontent.

Akhenaton's rule had not been the idyll that was conjured up in art. Reality lay in the hunger, suffering, and death beyond the borders of Aton's Horizon. In the eyes of all but the elite around him, pharaoh had wrecked society. As troops made up of foreign soldiers policed the land prohibiting the worship of every god but Aton, the Egyptian empire was being shaken to its foundations. The uneasy feeling that his revolution had failed probably plagued the last years of pharaoh's life. He died in year seventeen. By then Kiya had disappeared, as had Nefertiti.

Following pharaoh's death, Aton's Horizon was abandoned and avoided as a place of unspeakable heresy. The last of the inhabitants fled hastily and never looked behind them. Eating and drinking vessels were left on tables, children's playthings lay abandoned in the empty halls. Desert winds tore open the shutters, sand drifted over the floors, fish pools dried up, and fruit trees withered. The whole city decayed into ruins. It perished as rapidly as pharaoh had brought it to life.

Smenkara had passed away after a brief reign. The boy Tutankhaton was taken to Thebes and his name changed to Tutankhamun. Deep scars and a sense of shaken confidence pervaded Egypt. Superficially, the country returned to the traditional religion that had prevailed before Akhenaton, but in reality nothing could ever be the same again. On the good side, the new freedom in art lived on. In writing, the use of the vernacular had spread. It led to the development of new literary styles in the Ramesside Period. However, a dark, brooding mood hung in the air.

Unlike the other boy-kings of the Eighteenth Dynasty for whom their mothers acted as regents, Tutankhamun (1336–1327 BC) had no elder queen to look after him. The courtier Ay was appointed to act in his name as God's Father. Ay's policy was one of thorough and non-violent restoration. The young king was married to his half-sister Ankesenpa-aton, renamed

Ankhesenamun. The residence was moved to Memphis, but Thebes remained a religious center, "the southern Heliopolis," to satisfy the High Priest of Amun. It remained the burial ground for kings until the end of the New Kingdom.

General Horemhab continued to command the army. Maya, the "overseer of the king's treasury," was sent on a mission to demolish the temples and palaces of the former regime. Maya probably organized the transfer of the mortal remains of the royal family from Aton's Horizon to Thebes. From Memphis, Tutankhamun issued the Restoration Decree that reinstated all the traditional cults.

The people could now return to their faith. A major campaign to rebuild the temples and reorganize the clerical administration was set in motion. The army resumed its forays to Syria, encountering the Hittites, the new military power from Anatolia. These skirmishes had failed to establish a new balance of power. On the other hand, reasserting Egyptian authority in Nubia was more successful. With Horemhab, Egypt was back in the military arena.

The events surrounding the death of young Tutankhamun are far from clear. The king died unexpectedly in his tenth regnal year. The same year Horemhab led a military expedition against the Hittites at Amqa in Syria that ended in Egyptian defeat. By the time news of this disaster reached Egypt, Tutankhamun was dead. The funeral was conducted by the aged Ay, who also assumed the throne (1327–1323 BC). He had appropriated the royal tomb for himself, hastily burying Tutankhamun in a small, makeshift grave that could barely contain the quantities of goods customary to a king. Sheer chance preserved this improvised burial for posterity.

Since Ay had no male heir, he designated general Horemhab as his successor. It may have been at this point that the widowed Ankhesenamun, Akhenaton's daughter, took the bold step of writing to the Hittite king, prompted by fear, as she said in her letter.[2] She asked him to make one of his sons her husband in order that "Egypt and Hatti become one country." This extraordinary step met with suspicion in the Hittite capital and the king hesitated. In the end, he decided to dispatch his son Zananza to Egypt, but the unfortunate prince was murdered on the way. The result was prolonged warfare with the Hittites.

Who was Ankhesenamun afraid of? A fragmentary cuneiform letter from Ay suggests that he tried to make amends with the Hittites, denying all responsibility for the death of the prince. Backtracking on his earlier decision, he also made an effort to prevent Horemhab from becoming king after his own death, appointing the army commander Nakhtmin (possibly a grandson) as heir. Shortly thereafter, he died. Despite Ay's efforts, Horemhab succeeded in mounting the Egyptian throne and despoiling the tombs of both Ay and Nakhmin. Ankhesenamun and her sisters were heard of no more. Though riddled with difficulties, the general's path to the throne could not be stopped. In his salient Coronation Stele, Horemhab claimed kingship through the divine oracle of Horus of Hutnesu (probably his birthplace) in the tradition of the Thutmoside kings.

By comparison to his dramatic rise to the throne, Horemhab's reign (1323–1295 BC) appears uneventful. Even its exact length is not clear; in inscriptions, he counted his predecessor's rule as his own. His highest attested regnal year in Egypt is thirteen; Babylonian chronology, as well as two posthumous texts, indicated that he ruled longer.

Horemhab had been married to Mutnedjmet, whose only known title was the ordinary "songstress of Amun," but the couple had no children. As heir he chose Paramessu, the commander of the fortress at Sile on the land bridge to Syria, possibly preoccupied with reorganizing the army in the north.

Paramessu's family came from Avaris, the former capital of the Hyksos. When Horemhab died, Paramessu became king Ramses I (1295–1294 BC). The throne of Egypt was firmly in the hands of the army. With the end of the Eighteenth Dynasty history had come full circle. Avaris rose up from the ashes while Thebes was never to be the capital of Egypt again. The divine ancestor of the Ramesside kings was Seth. Avaris became the new residence of the Ramesside rulers.

Ramses I was probably old when he was made king, with a son and grandson already born to him. His reign lasted for barely a year, during which his son Sety was appointed commander of Sile, vizier and High Priest of Seth. In a few months, he was king (1294–1279 BC).

If Ay can be called the architect of the restoration, Sety was undoubtedly its master builder. His entire reign epitomized a commitment to the recovery of the faith lost in the censorship and iconoclasm of Akhenaton. Everywhere, inscriptions and images hacked out by Akhenaton's agents were re-carved. At Thebes, the festival of Amun, the Beautiful Feast of the Valley, was reinstated. At Abydos, a magnificent new temple complex recreated the mythical burial of Osiris. Sety's dedicatory inscription listed all the former kings of Egypt; the list had Horemhab directly succeeding Amenhotep III. Akhenaton, Ay, and Tutankhamun were left out.

Most impressive of all were Sety's attempts to resolve the crisis in religious thinking that was a direct result of Akhenaton's monotheism. Steeped as we are in centuries of monotheistic thinking we might easily underrate the theological achievement of Akhenaton. He was a true reformer. He has been called "the first individual in history."[3] His single creed introduced a semblance of order into an otherwise chaotic religious legacy. His historical importance is incontestable; centuries later, his thought and poetry would continue to inspire religions that were to follow.

The polytheistic religion of Egypt had come from many different sources. There were several creator-gods and creation myths. Temple establishments had maintained their independence, taken care of their own traditions, and looked after their own interests. Depending on the political climate, their influence rose and fell. Religious life relied on ritual and cult rather than on ordered religious thought. Faith was often manipulated to suit the purpose of the rulers, superstition and magic reigned unfettered, and priests had the sole authority to define truths. Tombs were granted only to those who were obedient to the king and papyri sold to the credulous like papal indulgences to exonerate them in the next world. In the midst of this, Akhenaton had raised the question of the One True and Living God. He had obliterated the social and religious hierarchy, at least in theory, and placed all people in humility before the sole creator. In fact, it had become impossible to relapse into the old familiar beliefs without attempting a religious reformation.

Sety tried to reconcile the contradictions that now glared at everyone. He encouraged theologians to probe more deeply into ancient dogmas and unite them into a single, respectable system of beliefs. The results of this rethinking were evident both in the temple complex at Abydos and in Sety's tomb in the Valley of the Kings. The former made the attempt to transform the religion of Osiris into a universal creed. The latter contained the most complete rendition of all the existing Books of the Afterlife. Their layout within the tomb reflected the attempt to treat them as a distinct body of religious texts. These two monuments presented new religious ideas that united the old with the new, the One with the Many. Sety's monuments became blueprints. The theological reconciliation offered by the religious thinkers of his time was scrupulously followed until the end of the New Kingdom.

It was possibly from Akhenaton's verse – "you are one, yet a million lives are in you" – that the Ramesside designation of a new all-god, "the one who made himself into millions," was coined. This formula was probably the precursor of the Hermetic *hen kai pan*, the concept of god as one and all, developed in Greco-Roman Egypt.[4] Akhenaton's ideas lived on. Through Hermetic philosophy they eventually influenced much of early Christian thought.

Sety died in year eleven, to be succeeded by his son Ramses II (1279–1213 BC). The latter had little of his father's imagination and depth of insight. What he lacked in acumen he made up for in pride. During his long reign of sixty-seven years, Ramses II set out to break every record. Though kings usually remained content with one principal wife, he married two. The first, Nefertari, received the most magnificent tomb in the Valley of the Queens and a rock-cut temple at Abu Simbel. The second, Isis-nofret, was the mother of his preferred children. In addition, he had a sumptuous harem and fathered more than fifty sons.

Plate 1a The step pyramid of Djoser at Saqqara in 1907. Courtesy of Lehnert and Landrock Bookshop and Gallery, Cairo

Plate 1b The pyramids of Giza during the flood in 1923. Courtesy of Lehnert and Landrock Bookshop and Gallery, Cairo

Plate 2   The Narmer palette, ca. 3100 BC. Courtesy of the Egyptian Museum, Cairo

Plate 3   Seated scribe, ca. 2494–2345 BC. Courtesy of the Egyptian Museum, Cairo

Plate 4 Detail of a colossal statue of Akhenaton, 1352–1336 BC. Courtesy of the Egyptian Museum, Cairo

Plate 5 Detail of the wooden coffin of Ramses II, showing the king with the divine beard, crook, and flail of Osiris, 1279–1213 BC. Courtesy of the Egyptian Museum, Cairo

Plate 6   Back of the throne of Tutankhamun, 1336–1327 BC. Courtesy of the Egyptian Museum, Cairo

Plate 7   Face of a goddess, shrine of Tutankhamun, 1336–1327 BC. Courtesy of the Egyptian Museum, Cairo

Plate 8a Boat and Sailors, the tomb of Menna, Luxor West, ca. 1390 BC. Author's photograph

Plate 8b Plowing in the fields of peace, the tomb of Sennedjem, Luxor West, ca. 1279–1213 BC. Author's photograph

His first campaign to Nubia took place while he was still co-regent with Sety and he took two of his stripling sons along. His first Asiatic campaign in year four led to the annexation of Amurru, with Egyptian influence extending once more as far as Ugarit. In return, the Hittites retaliated with all their military might. The ensuing battle of Khadesh that took place the following year was subsequently described in a long epic poem, the first one of its kind, that decorated nearly all of the king's prolific monuments. This single event had allowed the king to prove his courage and resolve. It also created the opportunity for endless self-promotion.

The sequence of events was as follows: Ramses had made a quick advance on Khadesh with only one of his four divisions, believing reports that the Hittite king was far away in Tunip. Suddenly, his chariots were stormed by the bulk of the Hittite army. The Hittite king had ambushed the following second division, cutting Ramses off from the others. Now he tried to crush him. Hopelessly outnumbered, the Egyptians began to flee. When even his immediate bodyguard were ready to desert him, Ramses called out to his father Amun and fought the attackers almost single-handedly. Amun had heard his call and intervened. In the nick of time a support force from the second division had come to his rescue, attacking the Hittites from the rear. With the arrival of the third division at sunset, the Egyptians were able to reassemble their forces. The following day the two armies clashed again, but the battle ended in stalemate. Truce was agreed, but Ramses declined the Hittite offer of peace.

Antagonism followed for several more years. At last, the oldest known peace treaty in history was signed. Negotiated in November of 1259 BC, it was written on silver tablets in both Akkadian and Egyptian. It put an end to hostilities between the two powers, obligated them to mutual military assistance in the event of rebellion or enemy attack, and arranged for the return of political fugitives. Though the two kings were equals, the Hittite king still complained that Ramses treated him "like a subject." A boundary was established on the basis of the status quo, with a portion of Amurru going to the Egyptians and Khadesh to the Hittites.

Both parties scrupulously adhered to the treaty. Their rather cool relationship underwent gradual warming. The Hittite king was invited on a state visit to Egypt. He became ill. Then followed prolonged negotiations for a dynastic marriage. Double correspondence was carried out between the kings and the queens. The Hittite king, who suffered from an eye ailment, was in need of Egyptian doctors and medicine. He also wanted a cure for his sterile sister.

At last a Hittite princess was dispatched and conducted to Egypt with all due pomp in the winter of 1246–1245 BC. The official account of this "miraculous" event was recorded on many temples throughout the land. Egyptians and Hittites were represented fraternizing in joint banquets. Another Hittite princess entered the king's harem. The treaty had brought decades of peace.

The building projects of Ramses II were immense. It seems that having the pyramids as the standard against which to measure their own achievements, many kings of Egypt were doomed to overextend themselves. None more so than Ramses II. The site of Per Ramses near Avaris, the biblical Piramses, the subject of many a wail of the children of Israel in the Book of Exodus, grew from the dwelling quarters of his father to include a series of splendid temples adorned with sphinxes, obelisks, and statues. When enough could not be procured, other monuments were usurped.

Every site in the Nile valley received lavish additions inscribed with the king's ubiquitous names. Particularly impressive were eight rock-cut temples in Nubia, two of them at Abu Simbel, probably built by a workforce rounded up from among the local tribes. Following in the footsteps of Amenhotep III, the king had a pronounced penchant for the colossal.

Although architects, sculptors, and masons tried to maintain a high quality of work, they were often faced with impossible commissions of dozens of colossi and miles of relief. As a result, many of the monuments, especially those from the later part of the reign, exhibit a lack of creative originality and a somewhat coarse execution. A movement from elegant slenderness to awkward bulk can be seen in columns and statues. In relief, the faster, more economical technique of sunk relief replaced almost entirely the art of raised relief. The king went for size and quantity.

Already, during the eighth year of his reign, Ramses had himself deified and his name written as "Ramses-the-god." His colossal statues were set up in front of all the great temples, becoming objects of public worship and receiving regular cult offerings. Two of these colossi still greet the modern visitor to Cairo on the way from the airport in Heliopolis. Another stands in front of the railway station. Within temples, Ramses-the-god had his own cult image and processional barge. In temple sanctums he was worshiped in the brotherly embrace of other gods. In reliefs, Ramses the king was often shown giving offerings to Ramses-the-god.

Among the king's numerous children Khaemwaset stood out. When he came of age, he was installed as High Priest of Ptah in Memphis. He initiated the Sarapeum, the underground gallery tomb of the Apis bulls, and was entrusted with numerous building projects in the Delta. Khaemwaset seems to have had a genuine interest in literature and art, restored many Old Kingdom monuments, and was probably one of the champions of copying the great literature of the past. He became the hero of several adventure stories that presented him as a great magician by the name of Setne Khaemwas. In one story, Setne went in search of the sacred Book of Thoth. In another, his father

Ramses II was magically transported to Nubia where he was afflicted with five hundred blows of the whip. Thoth was obliged to intervene personally to help the Egyptians get revenge by doing the same to the Nubian chief.

New compositions, such as mythical stories, folk tales, and love poetry that sprang up from the oral tradition, were recorded in the vernacular language, officially introduced by Akhenaton. It was said on a Ramesside papyrus that the only immortality one could expect was the immortality of the written word. One of Ramses' colossal statues set up by Khaemwaset still lies in the meager remains of ancient Memphis (Mit Rahina). It was so large and heavy that it could not be lifted up; instead, a two-story museum was built around its recumbent remains. The people of the near-by village still believe that this virile image has the power of endowing women with children.

Ramses II was the longest reigning monarch since Pepy II of the Old Kingdom. During the last years of his life he had become a living legend. His memory endured for thousands of years and was often confounded with that of the other kings whose monuments he so avidly usurped. Twelve sons had predeceased him, and it was the thirteenth, Merenptah, the fourth son of Isis-nofret, already an aged man, who eventually succeeded him.

Merenptah (1213–1203 BC) was best known to history for encountering the so-called "People of the Sea." At this time, drought and famine in the Mediterranean region had caused numerous migrations of people and they now menaced all the states in the Near East. The Sherden, who later gave their name to Sardinia, the Shekel who settled in Sicily, the Luka (Lycians), the Peleset (Philistines), and the Tursha (possibly Etruscans), described as Sea Peoples by the Egyptians, had made an alliance with the Libyan tribes. Together, they launched an attack on Egypt. Their strength lay in the use of new iron weapons that had changed the technology of warfare.

Merenptah's army faced the Sea Peoples in the western Delta near Buto and beat them back in a bloody six-hour battle that reportedly cost the enemy more than eight thousand dead. This achievement was commemorated on the Victory Stele that mentioned in the same breath the expedition against Cana'an, Askalon, Gezer, and the people of Israel in the eastern provinces. It remained the only reference to the people of Israel in Egyptian records.

Not having much time to build his tomb and funerary temple in Thebes, Merenptah pillaged the funerary temple of Amenhotep III for statues, relief, and stone blocks. This was the beginning of its steady demolition. After Merenptah's death in year ten, trouble over the succession broke out. Although the next king, Sety II (1200–1194 BC), was almost certainly the eldest son of Merenptah, a rival king Amenmesses ruled for a few years in the south. At some point, Sety II succeeded in erasing all of the latter's inscriptions and destroying his unfinished tomb.[5]

Sety II died after a reign of six years, succeeded by his only son with a Syrian concubine, Siptah (1194–1188 BC), a sickly young boy with an atrophied leg who ruled for no more than six years. In the meantime, Sety's widow Tausert, the boy's stepmother, had adopted a favorite, a Syrian official who became "Chancellor of all the Land." After Siptah'death, Tausert ruled for two more years, (1188–1186 BC), the third queen on the Egyptian throne after Sobek-Neferu and Hatshepsut. With her, the Nineteenth Dynasty came to an end.

It remains unclear how the Twentieth Dynasty came to power. It seems that after the death of queen Tausert, her Syrian consort had held on to power until he was expelled some two years later. Setnakht died soon after establishing the new dynasty. He was followed by his son Ramses III (1184–1153 BC). In an attempt to steady the swaying fortunes of his time, Ramses III tried to emulate his namesake Ramses II in every way. He copied his throne name and his funerary temple and even gave the names of the children of Ramses II to his own children. Eventually, all his successors were called Ramses, since this royal name had become synonymous with kingship, like Caesar's in the Roman empire.

However, times had changed irrevocably. The mighty Hittite kingdom had been utterly destroyed by the Sea Peoples, its capital sacked and ravaged. The same fate fell upon Cyprus, Ugarit, Tarsus, Amurru, and Allalakh. The Homeric Greeks overran the Mycenean sites in Greece. New tribes had settled in northern Syria. The Iron Age had stormed in.

In year eight of Ramses III, the Sea Peoples launched another attack by land and by sea on the Egyptian kingdom. Major sea-battle and army engagements followed. The Egyptian army was still powerful enough to halt their advance, but the Mediterranean world was transformed for good.

Ramses III did his best to continue as before. He built a great temple at Medinet Habu in western Thebes. He added two small temples to Karnak and built a tomb in the Valley of the Kings. But exhaustion and lack of resources plagued his entire reign. His buildings were made of reused stone, the reliefs were done in haste and did not fit properly, and the art was devoid of inspiration.

In year twenty-eight the first organized strike in history took place. The workmen of Deir el Medina who built the monuments on the west bank staged a march on the administration after their payments had been withheld for two months.[6] Raids by groups of Libyan nomads in the western desert reached as far as Thebes.

A general sense of insecurity pervaded the kingdom. Ramses III held on for nearly thirty-one years; in the end, he perished as victim of a conspiracy during the celebration of the annual festival of Amun at Thebes, the Beautiful

Feast of the Valley. As Amun's bark arrived at Medinet Habu and everyone gathered to watch the procession, conspirators led by prince Pentawer and his mother Tiy struck the aged king. Their murderous scheme had included smuggling wax figures and magical spells into the harem.[7] Before they could finish off pharaoh they were intercepted, but the king died soon afterwards. Ramses IV (1153–1147 BC) succeeded to the throne and brought the conspirators to trial. The guilty were required to commit suicide, their minors sentenced to have their noses and ears cut off.

After the rule of Ramses III Egypt lost all its provinces in Syria and Palestine. Eight more kings by the name of Ramses followed Ramses III. They ruled with ever diminishing prestige and power. In the reign of Ramses VII (1136–1129 BC) grain prices soared to their highest level. The first robberies of the Theban Necropolis and temples took place in the reign of Ramses IX (1126–1108 BC). Some thieves were apprehended and stood trial. Others got away with it. By the rule of Ramses XI (1099–1069 BC) crisis had turned into despair. Libyan gangs prevented the workers of Deir el Medina from going to work, tomb robberies continued, and the population was gripped by famine during "the year of the hyenas."

Some time around year twelve of Ramses XI, the viceroy of Nubia Panehesy appeared at Thebes with his Nubian troops to restore law and order, possibly at the request of pharaoh. He was given the title "overseer of the granaries" to feed his men. This brought him into conflict with the High Priest. The conflict escalated and soon the High Priest was besieged by the Nubian troops at Medinet Habu. Civil war followed. Panehesy marched north, where the general Piankh and his army intercepted him. With Panehesy forced to withdraw to Nubia, power fell into the hands of Piankh. The latter took over Panehesy's titles as well as those of the High Priest of Amun. His rule had all the trademarks of a military coup.

Piankh settled at Thebes. For gold, he began pillaging the royal tombs in the Valley of the Kings. This practice was continued by his successors. It took almost a century to empty out the royal tombs. Even the mummies of the great pharaohs of the New Kingdom were rewrapped to strip their bodies of amulets. At the end, their remains were buried in an anonymous tomb in the Theban cliffs.

Ironically, the only royal mummies that escaped this fate were those of Akhenaton and Tutankhamun, the heretic father and his "reformed" son, whose provisional burials had not been found by the High Priest and his agents. Theirs are the only royal golden sarcophagi of the New Kingdom that have survived for posterity. Akhenaton's gold casket had been despoiled, its face torn off, possibly on the occasion of his re-burial at Thebes. At the foot of the casket, written in gold, was a short poem:

> That I breathe the sweet air that issues from your mouth,
> that I behold your beauty every day – that is my prayer.
> That I hear your voice in the north breeze,
> that my body be instilled with life through your love.
> That you extend your hands to me, bearing my sustenance
> and that I receive it and live by it.
> That you call my name again and again,
> and that I never cease to answer.[8]

By chance, the lavish provisions of Tutankhamun have survived almost intact. They were discovered by Howard Carter in 1922 and are still the most vivid reminder of Egypt's golden pharaohs (plates 6 and 7). The imperial era was over.

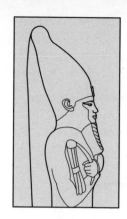

CHAPTER 8

BOOKS OF THE AFTERLIFE

The scribe Ani, who lived in the Ramesside Period, late enough to have experienced the intricacies of theocratic politics, diplomatically threw his faith into the hands of both Osiris and Ra in his custom-made Book of the Dead. The papyrus began with a hymn to Ra, in which Ani prayed that Ra's boat of millions of years would pick him up at the gates of sunset, carry him through the netherworld, and drop him off at the fields of peace. Ani's prayers to Osiris contained a chapter on "not rotting," a chapter on "not perishing," and two chapters on "not dying a second time." The Egyptians of Ani's time shrewdly reasoned that not only must there be life after death, but also there must be death after death as well.[1] New Kingdom literature teemed with mysticism, religious speculation, and myth.

Even before Akhenaton, religion had taken a new turn. One development that the New Kingdom rulers encouraged was the revival of the cult of Ra. They were looking for precedents. The patron of the Old Kingdom pharaohs was the only god who could match Amun, the new royal icon. As Amun-Ra he was now entitled to Ra's heritage.

The stories of Ra, probably kept alive at the temple in Heliopolis, were not only taken up but also given new interpretations. The somewhat self-conscious revival of the sun-cult can be seen in such compositions as the Litany of Ra, written in the form of a eulogy. In it, the court poet dutifully spelled out the seventy-five designations of Ra for the benefit of the king in the next world.

The Book of the Heavenly Cow also came from Heliopolis (figure 8.1). It described Ra's punishment of the human race for their rebellion against him. In his old age Ra was grieved by the decline of respect for him in the world he had created, especially among people, the fruit of his own tears. His human creations laughed at him, saying: "Look at Ra! He is old!" He was angered by their ridicule and wanted to teach them a lesson. "Summon here my daughter

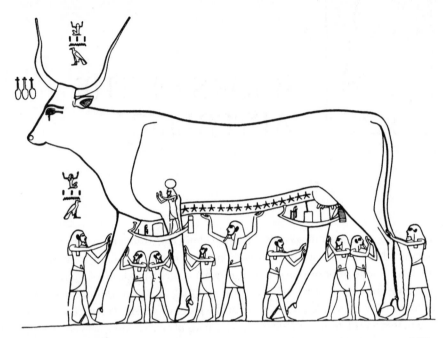

Figure 8.1   The heavenly cow, tomb of Sety I, 1294–1279 BC. After Hornung, 110

Hathor and all the gods who dwell in the great ocean of the sky!" he commanded. All the gods and goddesses assembled at the mansion of Ra in the Hidden Place. They bowed before him and asked their creator what he wanted them to do. Ra addressed the oldest of the gods, the primeval ocean Noun: "Behold the men I have created, how they speak against me! Tell me what you think I should do to them!" Noun suggested that he send Hathor to kill all those who attacked him.

Hathor assumed the form of a fierce lioness and went to seek revenge. She told people that they should not laugh at the creator and shed blood throughout the land. Soon, she took delight in slaughter. Ra was pleased: "Come in peace, Hathor! Have you not done what I have asked you to do?" But the goddess couldn't stop her rampage. For many nights the waters of the Nile ran red with the blood of mortals and Hathor's feet became crimson. Now Ra became afraid that she would eliminate the entire human race and he took pity on people. He sent his swiftest messengers to Elephantine Island at Assuan to fetch the fruit of the mandrake, a plant that causes drowsiness. Its fruit is crimson and its juice blood red. All night his servants crushed barley and mandrake together to make a red-colored beer. They made 7,000 measures of red beer and finished the task just as dawn broke. Ra told the gods that he had found the way to save humankind and sent his messengers to spread the drink all over the earth.

Hathor arose and set out to continue her task. She passed through the land looking for more pray, but saw none. Instead, she saw the earth steeped in the red liquid. She stooped to drink from it and the more she drank, the more she wanted. At last, she sank into a slumber. Her mind was happy and her limbs tired. Ra commanded that in the future this event should be celebrated in the city of Amun and for generations the followers of Hathor worshiped the goddess by drinking beer. Then, on the back of the heavenly cow, Ra retreated to heaven.

The fall of humankind abolished the Golden Age established at the dawn of creation. In the new age, Ra reordered the world. He separated night from day, people from gods, and heaven from the netherworld. For people, the original paradise was lost; strife and death came into the world. They had to try to overcome their fall and try to regain the original unity.

Rebirth was a different matter. From the Middle Kingdom on, it had been the exclusive prerogative of Osiris and his tribunal. Thus, reconciliation between the heaven of Ra and the underworld of Osiris was in order. During the reign of Amenhotep I an entirely new literary genre developed with the Book of What is in the Netherworld, or *Amduat*. Within a few generations several more books of similar content appeared in royal tombs: the Book of Gates, Spell of Twelve Caves, and Enigmatic Book of the Netherworld. Their mystical character was clearly expressed in their visual imagery – they teemed with obscure otherworldly beings. These books were reserved for tombs of kings; even queens were not allowed to use them.

The journey of the sun through the netherworld had become the favorite theme of the time. The Spell of Twelve Caves described the twelve unfathomable caverns of the netherworld inhabited by gods and genii of the infernum who either destroyed or granted favors to the dead. Celestial deities – *dei superi* – descended *ad infernum* to illuminate the restless souls. Ra granted to the dead the ability to see and the power to open the well-guarded gates of the world beneath.

The *Amduat* and the Book of Gates described the journey of the sun through the twelve hours of the night. In vignettes illustrating the scrolls of writing the netherworld was represented as the exact opposite of the world above: its gates and guardians stood upside down. When at sunset the boat of Ra sailed into this inverse world, it entered the body of Osiris, whose resurrective potencies were now put to work.

During the first hour the solar boat passed through a gateway called the Swallower of All. In the second and third hours it sailed through the land of abundance that contained the rejuvenating waters of Osiris. Ra distributed portions of land to the blessed dead, who carried ears of grain in their hands. In the fourth hour Ra met the goddesses of the hours and in the fifth, the timekeepers who looked after the measuring rope of time. Four races of men greeted him: the Egyptians, the desert dwellers, the dark Nubians, and the fair-skinned Libyans. In the sixth hour Ra encountered Osiris in the judgment hall. He permeated the body of Osiris and the two gods became the United One, a single deity that transcended all divisions. In the seventh hour Ra fought Apep, the serpent of darkness and oblivion. The force of light defeated the darkness, casting the serpent in fetters. In the eighth hour Ra raised the dead and in the ninth he subdued the enemies of Osiris, banishing them into pits of fire. In the tenth hour Ra encountered the souls of those who had drowned in the Nile. The water of the sacred river was a regenerating element that endowed all the drowned with a blessed posthumous existence. The eleventh hour was filled with preparations for the coming sunrise. It was crucial for time and the birth of the hours not to miss the moment of the sun's rebirth. All the primeval gods came to witness the twelfth hour, because every sunrise entailed the repetition of the first creation. The solar cycle, a mythical event of archetypal significance, took place outside time, but constantly through the timeless "present" of eternity. During his nightly descent to the underworld, the sun was renewed through his union with Osiris and born anew every morning in his new appearance. Having entered the tail of the snake as an old man, he emerged from its mouth as a youth.

The Spell of Twelve Caves, *Amduat*, and Book of Gates attempted to link the cult of Ra with the mythology of Osiris. The poetic reconciliation of the two opposing visions of the afterlife proved ingenious. During the nocturnal journey of the sun, the being of light and the lord of the depths met one another half way, blending into a single entity in the sixth hour of the night. The idea of resurrection through Osiris was thus identified with sunrise and the daily rebirth of the sun. The myth of Osiris had provided a metaphysics that perfectly complemented the celestial physics of Ra. As the solar agency of Ra helped to resurrect Osiris, so the netherworldly agency of Osiris helped the sun return to dawn after it passed through his body at nightfall. Even before Akhenaton, Egyptian religion had taken a few steps towards syncretism.

The tendency gained momentum after Akhenaton. A few more steps towards a religious settlement were evident in the inclusions of three gold masks for the mummy of Tutankhamun, a somewhat extravagant addition to the king's funerary equipment. While the king's three images were an allusion to the three bodies of Osiris, their golden aspect reflected the idea of enlightenment, illumination by the rays of the sun. The king's body was both Osiris and Ra, in form and essence.

The Enigmatic Book of the Netherworld, found on one of the gilded shrines of Tutankhamun, has no other parallels. Much of the text was written in the cryptographic script of the New Kingdom and was clearly regarded as esoteric. Those portions of the text that were written in hieroglyphs came from the Book of the Dead. The book has been interpreted as describing the "filling up" of the sun through the mystical union with Osiris during the night.[2] It is here that the ouroboros serpent – a snake biting its own tail – made its first appearance. The Egyptians called it simply "tail-in-mouth." It was to have a rich career in Greek, Roman, and European art.

Clever and imaginative as they were, these writings applied only to the king. One wonders if there was a real link between the privileged, the educated, and the common folk of Thebes. The temple of Amun, as it grew in size, surrounded itself with high walls that shut the people out. The only sacred writings dispensed to commoners were magical spells from the Book of the Dead, peddled outside the temple walls for a handsome fee. Their possession was an act of simple piety, and it ensured that the dead would reach the Land of the West. It is perhaps telling that none of the spells from the Book of the Dead written out on papyri, winding sheets, mummy bandages, amulets, or shards of pottery were exactly the same. Not two of the dead men's books were alike.

The Book of the Dead was essentially a collection of spells that served both as a guidebook to the unearthly topographies of the dark world and as a catalogue of verbal talismans to ward off hostile demons lurking in the shadows. There was no real plot. In the words of James Joyce, who used the Book of the Dead as a model for his novel *Finnegans Wake*, a reader who examined the Book of the Dead expecting to find a gripping story would in the end "go and hang himself." The book was more like a "passport" for the dead, written proof that they had chosen to immerse their souls in the fountains of remembrance and not forgetfulness.

On the journey between the slumber of death and the awakened consciousness, the dead had to undergo a number of "transformations." Among other things, they had to battle with inertia and the linens that swaddled them, drift their way through the kingdom of night while fending off nightmarish visions, and escape thirst and hunger by subsisting on images of food and water. At crucial points, they were expected to refer to appropriate chapters of their book and recite the necessary "words of power."

Whether they hoped to escape from danger, rise toward the boat of Ra, or fly to the house of Osiris, the prepared Egyptians found it advisable to include in their book spells that would enable them to turn into a hawk, heron, swallow, serpent, crocodile, and phoenix. "I fly like a hawk, I cackle like a goose . . . I advance to the realm of the star gods. The doors of Ma'at are open to me . . . I rise up like Ra . . . my heart, once brought low, is now made strong. I am a spirit in heaven, and mighty upon earth!"

When uttering the words "My heart! My mother! My coming forth from darkness!" the dead proved that they had advanced one step closer toward resurrection. With their mouths opened they breathed, sensed the presence of their hearts, and remembered their names. If all went well, the awakened souls reached the fields of peace – a better Egypt, where the sun shone anew every morning, the wheat grew taller, people did not have to work so painfully, and no one ever died (plate 8b).

Within this veritable web of charms and incantations we can glimpse the netherworld of the common man. It was divided into three parts: a sphere of light where the justified lived in a divine community centered around Osiris; a region of chaotic darkness where the damned suffered eternal punishment; and an area of "filtering" where the evil were caught in a net of doom. It paralleled the Heaven, Hell, and Purgatory of Christian teaching. Knowing the real nature of the components of the underworld endowed people with magical powers to avert the dangers.

The use of the Book of the Dead was prohibited under the iconoclasm of Akhenaton. When he died and a religious crisis gripped king and commoner alike, it was up to the theologians of Sety I to come up with a valid religious system. It is hardly surprising that they applied themselves first and foremost to the royal monuments. After all, the king set the example for all. More remarkable was Sety's prudent judgment in directing their efforts. He must have instinctively grasped the complexity of the situation he found himself in. The country required mending on many levels. Aside from securing the borders and reforming the army and the administration, the king was faced with the enraged clergy, not the least among them, the priesthood of Amun, who owned one fifth of the land of Egypt and its produce. They had been virtually put out of business by "the heretic."

Sety handled them with a steady hand. He built his tomb in the Valley of the Kings, following the established tradition. In choosing its content, he hearkened to the three major traditions of Egypt, that of Ptah of Memphis, Ra of Heliopolis, and Amun of Thebes. The cult of Osiris received a splendid temple at Abydos. By including all of them, Sety avoided favoritism; in weighing out the interests of many, he succeeded in restoring the balance of Ma'at.

Sety's tomb was the second largest in the Valley of the Kings after the unfinished tomb of Horemhab, the man who brought him to power. It followed the plan of the tomb of Horemhab. Every available wall surface was used for decoration, including doorjambs, corridors, and ceilings. All the Books of the Afterlife were written out in their most complete form. Homage was paid to the archaic ancestor cults (the souls of Pe and Nekhen), the rustic hymn to the eye of Horus, and the Opening of the Mouth ceremony of the Old Kingdom. The vaulted roof of the sarcophagus chamber was decorated with images of the constellations and the decan stars. In fact, it seems as if virtually all the available texts and temple records were utilized in decorating the tomb. The attention and care lavished on it were evident in the use of the most refined technique of raised relief to write and illustrate the texts. They were distributed around the tomb in such a way as to relate them to the king's journey in the hereafter, making them part of one story.

Having died, the king merged "with him out of whom he had come . . . Blended with the All, he is One and Many, he is god." His spirit followed the setting sun into the netherworld as seventy-five names of Ra were spoken for his protection. Sailing deeper into the night on Ra's boat of millions of years, the king descended past the gates of the hours of the night into the realm of Osiris. As the sun became one with Osiris, so the king's spirit tried to penetrate the god's essence. The rite of Opening the Mouth for Breathing was performed on Sety's statues to awaken his spirit. In the sarcophagus chamber, Sety's mummy was laid to rest under the vault of the night sky with its canopy of stars. The yellow-golden color of the sarcophagus chamber mirrored the original Golden Shrine where Ptah first fashioned the world. Then, through the narrow shaft below the sarcophagus, the king's soul descended still deeper to the waters of the primeval ocean. Having dissolved in the realm of chaos and darkness before creation he became an unborn child. Only then was he ready for new life. He was Osiris and Ra merged into one within the circle of eternal transformation. The sun could rise again above the boundless waters at the beginning of creation. The unfolding of life was ready to begin anew. Ascending, the king's spirit left the underworld and stepped forth into daylight, joining the eternal cosmic cycle.

Sety's tomb became a temple, the funeral mass a sacred litany of rebirth. It set the standards for generations to come. Members of the royal family and priests performed the newly fashioned rites during the king's funeral. Sety's son Ramses II was shown participating in the Opening the Mouth ceremony. As heir to the throne, he played the part of Horus to his deceased father Osiris-Sety. The funeral rites ensured Sety's passage through the underworld to heaven; surrounded by sacred texts and living images on the walls of his own temple of rebirth, the king's spirit traveled the eternal worlds on its timeless journey.

Many of the motifs in the tomb of Sety simply followed earlier precedents where the cult of Ra and the myth of Osiris had already clasped hands. The idea of spiritual resurrection as sunrise – enlightenment – and the concept of the sun god as the trinity of Atum-Ra-Khepri, three-in-one, had both come from the same source in Heliopolis. Even before Sety, the solar trinity was linked to the three bodies of Osiris in the gold masks of Tutankhamun. What was new here was the deliberate association of all the ancient traditions and the reference to the Memphite theology of Ptah in the same breath. In Sety's tomb the three most important religious traditions of Egypt were entwined as the answer to Akhenaton's monotheism. If some motifs had been freely associated before, it had now become imperative to affirm their relationship in writing and ritual.

The temple in Abydos was even more impressive in its articulation of the ancient cults. In its special arrangement it differed considerably from all the Theban temples, including Sety's own funerary temple in western Thebes. It was a unique creation that may have followed the wishes of Sety himself. It was called the "House of Millions of Years of King Men-Ma'at-Ra" (Sety I) who is contented in Abydos.

At the back of the temple was a cenotaph – a symbolic tomb – that reproduced in its architecture the mythical tomb of Osiris floating on a sub-terranean island surrounded by water. This fantastic vision was conjured up with the help of underground canals that conducted the water from a natural underground source. It is reminiscent of the Osiris shaft, built under the Khafra causeway at Giza some time during the New Kingdom.

The entrance of the temple was on the east side; all the chapels faced west. As a rule, Egyptian temples had one main chapel (holy of holies). At Abydos, seven chapels of equal importance placed side by side formed the nucleus of the temple. In a south–north sequence (the direction in which the Nile flows) lay the adjacent abodes of Sety, Ptah, Ra, Amun, Osiris, Isis, and Horus. This septet can be roughly divided into three groups. First, the king; second, the main gods of the country, Ptah of Memphis, Ra of Heliopolis, and Amun of Thebes; and third, the gods of the Osirian saga represented as the trinity of Osiris, Isis, and Horus.

The trinity of Ptah, Ra, and Amun was also a unity that symbolized all the gods of the country. The concept of the triad suggested plurality; in Egyptian writing three lines denoted the grammatical plural.[3] Plutarch wrote: "We are accustomed to express 'many times' also as 'three times,' just as we say 'thrice blest' and 'bonds three times as many,' that is, innumerable."[4]

Within religious doctrine, the number three symbolized the three souls of god: name, appearance, and essence. The three-fold aspect of god was paralleled by the three souls of man. Amun, Ra, and Ptah represented all the gods of Egypt while being at the same time three aspects of one god. As a reaction to Akhenaton's monotheism, there developed a concept of the unity of the cosmos, of a single god who lay hidden in the multiplicity of things and whose name remained secret from both deities and humans. A Ramesside hymn expressed this explicitly: "Three are all the gods: Amun, Ra, and Ptah.

He who hides his name is Amun, he who is visible is Ra, and his body is Ptah." Last but not least, the king, a third element, joined the two divine triads. The new triad implied that all the gods of the country were united under the aegis of Sety.

The back wall of every chapel had a false door, an imitation of a door carved in stone that symbolized the passage between this world and the next, a common feature of tomb architecture since the Old Kingdom. Only the chapel of Osiris, number five in the sequence, had a real door that led at a right angle to a set of three more chapels with a sealed back room. This is where the Mysteries of Osiris took place.

The three "mystery" chapels reiterated the theme of the trinity of Osiris, Isis, and Horus. They probably contained statues and sacred relics associated with each of them. In the central chapel of Osiris the resurrection of the god was celebrated in rituals that hearkened back to the Middle Kingdom, if not before. The content of the rituals can be inferred from the wall reliefs, among them, an image of the dead Osiris lying on a bier. On both sides of the bier stand mourning women. Above Osiris's recumbent body hovers Isis in the form of a kite, receiving from the risen god the seed of his son. The resurrection of Osiris was represented as the sexual union of Osiris and Isis, the engendering of the savior-child.

From the very beginning, the myth of Osiris contained the measurement of time. Horus-the-child was conceived at the spring equinox, the time of harvest, and born at the winter solstice. In the temple of Sety, the ancient rustic cult was invested with new religious meaning. The unity of Osiris and Ra was underlined by the theme of the trinity. It is at this time that the worship of Osiris explicitly encompassed the doctrine of One in Three: the Resurrected Redeemer, the Holy Mother, and the Savior-Child.

The meaning of the sealed room at the back of the three chapels is of particular interest. As it had no doorway, it was a blind chamber that may have been opened at certain times and resealed. Did it contain the chest of Osiris? Judging by its position and lack of door it is possible that it was a "hidden chamber" where the earth body of Osiris was kept and replaced every year.

Sety's new presentation of Egyptian religion was indeed magnificent. Seen through the blossoming papyrus columns of the court, the seven chapels, when lit by lamps during service, probably appeared to the believer as the seven-fold menorah candlelight in front of the Ark of the Covenant, described in the Book of Exodus. Seven aspects of one divine being illuminated the eternal landscape of the papyrus thicket where the savior-child was born. Sealed behind them in a secret chamber lay the mystical essence of the sacrificed god.

With Sety, Egypt's place in the universe was restored. In its grand vision, the temple of Abydos created the feeling that gods, kings, and people lived in harmony. It anticipated the famous pronouncement of Hermes Trismegistus, the Greek incarnation of Thoth: "Are you not aware, Asclepius, that Egypt is the image of heaven, or rather, that it is a projection below of the order of things above? If the truth must be told, this land is indeed the temple of the whole world!"[5]

Sety's temple is still one of the most beautiful in Egypt. The elegance of the delicate raised relief with its subdued colors introduced a new formal restraint, consciously contrasted to the exaggerated outlines of the art of Akhenaton. In its day, the building was embellished with precious wood, metals, and dazzling jewels. When it came alive during celebrations it must have sparkled in splendor.

The religious importance of the temple is clear from records of the endowments allotted to it. It was financed by income from the gold mines of Nubia and given possession of fields, herds, and men. Several of Sety's decrees were aimed at safeguarding its economic power. It was exempt from interference by the state authorities and all infringements on its assets were severely punished. In the case of loss of cattle, the responsible official had to replace the damage with its ten-fold value. If anybody used the men working on the temple for other tasks, he was punished with a hundred strokes of the rod and five bleeding wounds. In some cases, corporal punishment was followed by loss of office and removal to the forced-labor unit.

Neither the temple nor the cenotaph was completed during the king's lifetime. Ramses II continued building it, as did Merenptah after him. Ramses wrote in an inscription that he made statues for his father, "the most beautiful one for Abydos, the region which he loved and for which he longed ever since he lived on earth."

With their religion so gloriously redeemed, the people of Egypt could breathe a sigh of relief. They continued their burial practices, providing their dead with all the goods they could afford. By the lifetime of the scribe Ani, wealthy Egyptians commissioned their own, personalized Books of the Dead. They probably consulted with priests about the specific content as avidly as one might with lawyers about working out the right insurance policy. At no other time had the Egyptians thought about their mortality with more persistence and intensity than in the late New Kingdom. They seem to have begun preparing for their deaths as soon as they began to think.

Through the priestly class ideas from the royal Books of the Afterlife had trickled down the social ladder. In Ani's papyrus, the myths of Osiris and Ra had become so interlinked that they could no longer be distinguished from one another. Both gods were indispensable for the awakening of the individual soul. As Osiris had become enlightened, so Ra had become humanized. The interdependence of these myths was suggested in the very form and verbal texture of Ani's Book of the Dead, where the hymn to Ra was immediately followed by the hymn to Osiris. It blurred the two figures so incessantly that it became impossible to tell whose resurrective movement toward dawn and whose descent into nocturnal darkness was the cause and effect of whom. Together, they suggested not only that people arose in the morning because the sun did, but also that the sun arose in the morning because some human, creative power was there to resurrect, wake up, and see it.

CHAPTER 9

TOWARD THE SUNSET

In the Late Period foreign conquest brought the dominance and isolation of Egypt to an end. The balance of power in the Mediterranean world had been remade and foreigners vied for the Egyptian throne time and again. As the ancient world became smaller the myth of Osiris traveled beyond the Nile valley to the shores of Phoenicia. The voyage of Isis to Byblos in search of Osiris's body probably entered the story at this time. The Phoenicians spread the cult of Osiris around the Mediterranean world: in popular lore he was equated with Adon, the Lord of Byblos. Isis and her child had an even bigger following: she came to be worshiped as the Primordial Virgin and her infant as the Savior of the World.

In Egypt itself people tried to hold on to Amun and the legacy of the New Kingdom. But times had changed and political fragmentation could not be overcome. An overall picture of the country is difficult to piece together. No king lists mention Dynasties Twenty-one to Twenty-five. To outward appearances, the kingdom was united under the Twenty-first Dynasty, but in reality control was divided between a line of kings in the north and a sequence of army commanders in the south. The southern army commander also held the post of High Priest of Amun. Thus, in theory, the country was a theocracy ruled by Amun himself. Amun's decisions were communicated by oracles. Oracular consultations were formalized in the Festival of the Divine Audience held at Karnak.

In the north, the city of Tanis (San el Hagar) was developed as the counterpart of Thebes, but its function remained symbolic. During the rule of the Twenty-second Dynasty (945–715 BC) the division of the two kingdoms persisted. The ruling family in the north was of Libyan descent; it had become influential through judicious marriages and close ties to the High Priests of Amun at Thebes. Only one of them, Sheshonq (945–924 BC) (the biblical Shishak, 1 Kings 14: 25–6), pursued an aggressive policy. He installed his son as High Priest and raided both Israel and Judah. Biblical tradition described him as arriving at the head of 1,200 chariots and blamed him for seizing the treasures of the Temple in Jerusalem. The campaign was probably launched in support of Jeroboam, a pretender for the throne of Judah, who had found refuge in Egypt. However, it remained the only Egyptian attempt to influence Middle Eastern affairs. Under Sheshonq's successors, some of whom ruled contemporaneously as Dynasty Twenty-three, relations reverted to commercial contacts.

The excessive influence of the High Priests of Amun at Thebes had a destabilizing influence on kingship. This is illustrated by the attempt of Sheshonq to legitimize his claim to the throne. Custom demanded that he perform the Osirian ancestor ritual on a statue of his father Nimrod at Abydos. But to do so, Sheshonq required the approval of Amun and his representative on earth, the High Priest. Thus, Nimrod's statue was introduced to Amun of Thebes, where the god through the medium of an oracle consented to have it put up at Abydos. Amun still held sway over the most ancient religious capital.

Some changes in the attitude to death and burial took place in the Libyan Period. Tomb structures were greatly simplified and burial paraphernalia reduced in number, possibly due to impoverished circumstances. Of the literary compositions the *Amduat* and the Litany of Ra were the most popular. Individual spells from the Book of the Dead were folded and hidden inside hollow statuettes of Osiris. But the use of funerary texts had steadily declined through the Twenty-first Dynasty and by the Twenty-second Dynasty it had come to an end. Funerary texts on coffins were reduced to little more that offering formulae and divine speeches.

In the eighth century BC, the rulers of Kush near the fourth cataract of the Nile in Sudan had emerged as strong contenders for power. Under Piy, the Kushite troops took Thebes without a struggle and the towns of Upper Egypt either rapidly capitulated or were easily captured. A fully centralized government, however, was not restored. Instead, the Kushite king ruled as overlord and permitted local rulers to remain in control of their fiefs. Shabako's successors, Shebitko, Taharko, and Tanwetamani (702–656 BC), were officially recognized as Dynasty Twenty-five. For the first and only time in history the kings of Kush ruled over Egypt.

In a swift and effective political move the kings of Kush abolished the post of the High Priest of Amun and installed their own daughters as Divine Consorts of the Theban god. Precedents for it had been found in the New Kingdom title of "God's Wife of Amun," held by the all-powerful royal women of the Eighteenth Dynasty. However, unlike in the New Kingdom, the king's daughters were now expected to remain celibate and to adopt their successors from among the royal family. This rule probably had a political dimension: the celibacy of the Divine Consorts meant that no rival sub-dynasties could arise and the adoption system persisted until the end of the Twenty-sixth Dynasty. In this way, the power of the Amun priesthood was placed in firm control of the crown.

The Kushites were enthusiastic champions of bringing back the ancient religious, literary, and artistic traditions of Egypt. In their ambition to reinvigorate the Egyptian kingdom they pursued an aggressive policy toward Egypt's commercial partners in Palestine. This brought them into direct confrontation with the mighty kingdom of Assyria. As a consequence, much of the rule of Taharko (690–664 BC) was occupied with the desperate struggle to defend Egypt from the Assyrian army. After the sack of Thebes by Ashurbanipal in 663 BC the last Kushite king was expelled from Egypt.

With Assyrian support Psamtek (664–610 BC) was installed as ruler at Sais in the Delta. The Assyrians saw this as the continuation of the old system of rule through local princes. Soon, however, they could not maintain their military strength so far from their own country. Psamtek exploited this situation and some time around 658 BC he received support from Gyges in Lydia and freed himself from Assyrian domination. Herodotus mentions that he had employed Carian and Ionian mercenaries to strengthen his army. The Greeks had entered Egyptian history as warriors and it is small wander that in the end they conquered Egypt.

By 660 BC Psamtek controlled the Delta. Backed by a strong military force, he began negotiating for unity. Local princes quickly saw the advantage of coming to an agreement. Psamtek's daughter Nitokret was officially adopted by the daughter of the last Kushite king and appointed Divine Consort of Amun at Thebes. By 656 BC Psamtek had succeeded in reuniting the whole country and reversing the trend of foreign domination for a brief time.

As Egyptian history moved away from theocracy, the cult of Amun waned and the redemptive figure of Osiris reemerged from under its shadow. It was in the Twenty-sixth Dynasty that a massive bier of gray granite was placed in Osiris's sepulcher at Abydos. Four hawks at the corners of the bier kept watch over the dead god. Isis, the kite, hovered above the recumbent figure, becoming impregnated with the savior-child. "There he lay, in an attitude which indicated in the plainest way that even in death his regenerative virtue was not extinct, but only suspended, ready to prove a source of life and fertility to the world when the opportunity should offer."[1] The afterlife of Osiris was destined to continue. The seasonal festival at Abydos was resumed, but the ritual replacing of the chest of Osiris would not have been possible once the granite bier was installed in the tomb. It may have moved to the temple of Sety I.

With political decentralization, however, the role of Abydos as the center of the ancestor cult declined. Most likely, royal patronage was at best uneven. Just like in the Predynastic Period, numerous places were venerated as the "tombs" of Osiris. "The body of Osiris," Plutarch wrote,

> is said to lie buried in many places; for they say that the small town of Thinis . . . alone contains the real Osiris, and that the wealthy and powerful among the Egyptians are buried mostly in Abydos, deeming it an honor to be buried near the body of Osiris. They say that Apis, who is the image of the soul of Osiris, is reared in Memphis where also his body lies . . . The island near Philae, it is said, is usually untrodden and unapproached by any man, and not even birds come down on it; but at one appointed time the priests cross over and sacrifice there to the dead god, laying garlands on the tomb.[2]

The cult of Osiris was dispersed from Abydos all over Egypt. Many rustic customs were probably adopted at this time, among them, hollowing out the trunk of a tree and making an image of Osiris from the wood thus obtained. The image was buried in the hollow of the tree like a corpse, kept for a year and burned at the appointed hour, and the ashes scattered over the river. Then a new image was made from a tree especially cultivated for the occasion. Eventually, the worship of Osiris in sacred trees had spread outside Egypt and it was said that a tamarisk tree had sprung at the place where his coffin landed on the Phoenician coast. It was so magnificent that the king of Byblos wanted to have it in his palace.

Plutarch described how Isis when she came to Byblos sat down dejected and tearful near a fountain. She spoke to no one except the queen's maids, whom she greeted and welcomed, plaiting their hair and breathing upon their skin a wonderful fragrance which emanated from her. When the queen, whose name some say was Astarte, saw her maids she was struck with longing for Isis, who breathed ambrosia; so Isis was sent for and became her friend. She took care of the queen's children and tried to heal the sickly one by making him immortal on a pyre of fire. One night the queen spied on Isis and screamed when she saw her child put into the fire. Only then did Isis reveal herself. She demanded the wooden pillar with Osiris's chest inside it that held the roof of the palace. She took it from beneath with utmost ease and proceeded to cut away the body. Then she covered it with linen and poured sweet oil upon it. "To this day," Plutarch wrote, "the people of Byblos venerate the wood which is in the temple of Isis."[3]

While foreigners threatened Egypt's independence, people held fast to their traditions. By the reign of Amasis (570–526 BC) agriculture had been revived with spectacular success. According to Herodotus: "It was said that the reign of Amasis was the most prosperous time that Egypt ever saw – the river was more liberal to the land, and the land brought forth more abundantly for the service of man than has ever been known before; while the number of inhabited cities was not less than twenty thousand."[4]

Relations with Greece played a major role. A steady infiltration of Greeks flowed through Egypt and Greek trading outposts were established all over the Delta, the largest of them at Naukratis, not far from the capital at Sais. Another Greek colony at Cyrene, on the Libyan seacoast, had become a major trading base. Near Cyrene, in the oasis of Siwa in the Libyan desert, a new temple was built in the Greek style. It came to be revered as a great oracle and had its own High Priest or Prophet attached to it. Upon conquering Egypt, Alexander of Macedon set off to consult it.

The new system of trade established by the rulers of Sais was soon upset by the rise of the Persian empire. Under Cambyses (525–522 BC) the Persians attacked Egypt and defeated the army of Psamtek III at the battle of Pelusium. Egypt fell under Persian rule and the Persians constituted the Twenty-seventh Dynasty.

Herodotus, who visited Egypt during the Persian period, noted a degree of xenophobia among the Egyptians. It may have given impetus to the repeated religious revivals and archaizing trends in the religion and art of the period. Animal cults were revived and often followed to excess. It was during the Late and Ptolemaic Periods that the catacombs at north Saqqara acquired four million mummified ibises, half a million hawks, and five hundred baboons. Such was the Egyptian reverence of sacred animals that Diodorus described how he saw with his own eyes the Alexandrian mob demand and secure the death of an official Roman envoy for accidentally killing a sacred cat. All this, remarked Diodorus, despite the fear the Egyptians felt of the Romans.[5]

Magical texts, statues, and figurines had become widely popular. Statues and stelae were inscribed with healing spells of all kinds. Magic could have its trivial uses, too. One magical spell gave the following instructions for use: "Take a cat and make into an Osiris by putting its body in water." Invocations were directed to the "cat-faced one."

Religious festivals were maintained and observed with strict regularity. Hathor of Dendera journeyed to marry Horus of Edfu, escorted by a whole flotilla of small boats. On the eighteenth day of the tenth month her statue was taken to sail upriver to the temple of Horus. The goddess and her followers made numerous stops on the way and reached Edfu on the day of the new moon at the end of summer. There, on the eve of the anniversary of Horus's victory over Seth, the statue of Horus came out of the temple to greet the goddess on the waters. A priest wearing a jackal mask performed the Opening of the Mouth ceremony on the divine images and the divine pair were presented with offerings of the first fruits. That night the couple spent alone in the birth-temple. Their "beauteous embrace" was celebrated by "drinking before the gods and spending the night gaily." After two weeks of merry-making, Hathor was returned to her temple at Dendera.

Herodotus described the festival of the cat-goddess Bastet at Bubastis in the Delta as a revelry where "more grape wine was consumed . . . than in the rest of the year besides." People reached Bubastis by boat,

> many of the women with castanets, which they strike, while some of the men pipe the whole time of the voyage; the remainder of the voyagers, male and female, sing the while and make the clapping with their hands. When they arrive opposite any of the towns upon the banks of the stream, they approach the shore and while some of the women continue to play and sing, others call aloud to the females of the place and load them with abuse, while a certain number dance, and some standing up uncover themselves. After proceeding in this way all along the river course, they reach Bubastis where they celebrate the feast with abundant sacrifices.[6]

He also described with alarm the ritual of Seth in the temple at Papremis. One group of priests carried a gold-plated wooden statue of Seth on a four-wheeled cart. They tried to gain admission to the temple, but were repelled by another group. A mock battle ensued, in which priests engaged each other with clubs. Herodotus believed that some were even killed, though he had been assured that all was done as part of a religious festival.

The cult of the Apis bull in Memphis was maintained in spite of endless changes of authority over the city. Throughout a succession of rulers, many of them foreign, burials of the sacred bulls in the Serapeum at Saqqara continued. Apis had become one of the most popular deities of the Late Period. Plutarch described the care with which the priests treated the bull: they washed him in special chambers within the temple precinct, since they believed that the waters of the Nile had a fattening effect on beasts, people, and gods alike. Apis had to be trim, have the right marks on his body, and appear with the adornments due to a god.

Herodotus recorded a story about Apis and the Persian king Cambyses that had mortally offended Egyptian religious sensibilities. Cambyses was so angered by the pomp of the yearly festival of the "appearance" of Apis, that he commanded the priests to bring Apis before him. He then tried to slay him, but missed his aim and wounded the bull in the thigh. He mocked the Egyptians for worshiping bulls, showing them that Apis bled like any other animal. The priests hastily took Apis to the stalls and ministered to his wound, but the bull bled to death. They prepared him for burial and buried him secretly in the vaults. In the aftermath of his crime, Cambyses was driven mad and killed his own brother and sister. Plutarch was told that the Persian king had dined on Apis with his friends. This, he thought, showed "the harshness and wickedness of his character," though he added at the end of the same passage that "superstition . . . is no less an evil than atheism."[7]

Persian rule was punctuated by repeated revolts and in 404 BC the flag of independence was raised again. Amyrtaios (404–399 BC) established the Twenty-eighth Dynasty and sixty years of confrontation followed. By now Egypt relied heavily on Greek mercenaries as well as native forces. Unfortunately, many were used in the civil wars at home. The last two native Egyptian dynasties were plagued by constant infighting where individual ambitions overruled ideological unity. All the rulers of the Twenty-ninth Dynasty were shortlived; the Thirtieth was established after a military coup. Nevertheless, both Nectanebo I and II (380–343 BC) were prolific builders who left their mark at many sacred sites in Egypt. It is from the reign of Nectanebo II, the last native Egyptian pharaoh, that we have an especially large number of magical texts.

By this time, the growing presence of women in religious life had encouraged the widespread worship of child-gods. Female priestly titles came to include those of "nurse" and "divine mother." Emphasis on the mother–child relationship encouraged the building of mamisi-chapels where the birth of the divine child was celebrated. In the temple of the "golden girl" Hathor at Dendera, the mamisi was used for the enactment of the thirteen-act mystery play about the birth of the golden calf. Hippolytus described how the mystic silence of the wordless revelation was broken only by the loud cry of the hierophant proclaiming the child's birth. The initiates themselves were specified as children.

On the chapel's reliefs the birth of the golden calf was related to the birth of Nectanebo I (380–362 BC), in the attempt to endow the latter with divine status. There were close links between the "mamisiac" cults and the attempt to revive divine kingship. Several rulers from Sheshonq to Taharko were depicted in temple reliefs as nude infants being suckled by Hathor and Bastet. Late Period kings, however, proved unable to enjoy divine status in quite the same way as their predecessors. Their position in the social hierarchy was akin to that of military ruler.

The worship of child-gods persisted for centuries. They had similar features that extended even across different cultures: their mothers were virgins who had conceived them miraculously, their births were mysterious, and they had to overcome life-threatening adversities. The virginity of the mother was an indelible part of the child's divinity. The Primordial Maiden was a primal being. Her virginity was not anthropomorphic but rather a quality of the unadulterated primal element that had given her birth. She was an archetype that united the possibilities of being born and giving birth, her own feminine aspect, as it were.

The child-gods possessed divine powers that enabled them to avert danger and heal the sick. They carried the world on their shoulders, they were "smaller than small and bigger than big," their footsteps were those of a giant even if they were miniscule in size. Infinitely big and infinitesimally small, the child-gods provided the link with the past and the promise of a future.

The cult of Isis and Horus-the-child was especially popular. Hundreds of bronze figurines of Isis nursing her infant found in temples and households became models for the Christian figures of the Virgin and child. Steadily, the story of Osiris had spread beyond Egypt and around the entire Mediterranean.

By now the feast of Adon – the Lord of Byblos – had assimilated distinct traits of the Nile myth. Its observance endured until late antiquity, when Cyril of Alexandria described it in the following passage:

> Every year, the people beyond the rivers in Ethiopia [Sudan] used to write a letter to the women of Byblos informing them that the lost and lamented Lord was found. This letter they enclosed in an earthen pot, which they sealed and sent floating down the river to the sea. The waves carried the pot to Byblos where ... it arrived at the time when Syrian women were weeping for their dead Lord. The pot was taken from the water and opened; the letter was read and the weeping women dried their tears, because the lost Lord was found.[8]

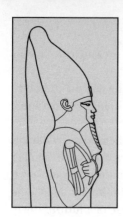

CHAPTER 10

GREEKS IN EGYPT

When the Greeks took over Egypt from the Persians they created a new god to rule supreme: Sarapis, a true Greco-Egyptian. His name was an amalgamation of Osiris and Apis and his countenance that of a mighty old Greek with a beard and bushy hair. A new temple was built to him in Alexandria and old rituals were adapted and elaborated to associate him with the Nile inundation.

Custom-made for the new rulers, Sarapis proved to be a lasting success. Shrines to him arose all over the Mediterranean world and his cult endured as a stronghold of paganism until late Roman times. The cult of Isis lasted even longer. The Greeks had appointed her Protector of Seafarers and her statue stood guard on the island of Pharos, at the entry to the port of Alexandria. She became the most popular deity of the classical world and even the advent of Christianity did not bring an end to her worship. Instead, Isis and her miraculous child were adopted by the new faith and lived on in the new world.

Alexander of Macedon (years of rule in Egypt 332–323 BC), known to history as Alexander the Great, had set out to defeat Persia, the traditional enemy of the Greeks. He succeeded in doing so in two great battles, one at Issus (Alexandretta) and another at Gaugamela on the Tigris. As soon as he conquered Syria, Egypt fell into his hands. He went to Memphis where, according to the semi-mythical biography the Alexander Romance, written anonymously some time around the second century AD under the pseudonym Callisthenes, he had himself crowned as pharaoh. Crowned or not, the Egyptians had eagerly endowed him with the traditional royal titles, for they too hated the Persians, and henceforth he showed great respect for Egyptian religious sensibilities.

In reality, Alexander initiated a period of thorough political change that had a terminal effect on the old ways. The Greeks had come to stay. Egyptian culture was to some degree enriched by the Hellenic influx. But it was also diluted and fragmented and lost much of its earlier confident originality and strength. During the three centuries of Greek rule (332–30 BC), Hellenization, particularly in language, took root in Egyptian society. In art, the old clarity was no longer there. Ultimately, the Greek and the Egyptian manners of representation clashed, and eventually the Egyptian canon gave way to Greek art. In religion, the Egyptian gods were deliberately merged with the Greek. But from now on, it was Greek thought that ruled the world. The mythical explanation of the Egyptian world no longer sufficed; the Greeks believed in reason.

Alexander had planned to include Egypt in the Greek empire. He sailed the Nile from Memphis to the northwestern coast, where he commissioned his architect Dinocrates to build a Greek city around the nucleus of the small Egyptian town of Rakotis. The people of Rakotis had been coastguards and goatherds. Their chief gods were Ra and Osiris. Their settlement gained in importance only after it had become a little lump of Egypt embedded in the new Greek city. Alexander's scheme combined idealism with utility. He needed a capital for his Egyptian kingdom that could be linked with Greece.

Having given his orders, the 23-year-old king hurried on to the oasis of Siwa and the oracle of Amun. At Siwa, the High Priest declared him a son of Amun and a god in his own right. Henceforth, his fate was sealed. On newly minted coins his image was adorned with the divine ram horns of Amun. Following providence, Alexander went on to conquer the world and never saw a single building rise in Alexandria. If he looked on it as a dream of his youth, little did he suspect that he would return to rest there eternally after his death in the heat of a Babylonian summer at the age of 33. Alexander was mummified Osiris-like in the Egyptian fashion.

In November of that same fateful year, Ptolemy Lagidus (son of Lagus), one of his most distinguished generals, arrived in Alexandria after shrewdly bargaining to obtain the position of governor. Ptolemy realized all the benefits that would proceed from the possession of Alexander's body. On his deathbed, Alexander had requested to be buried at Siwa, near his father Amun. After some vicissitudes, his body was brought to Memphis. There it rested until his mausoleum, the Soma, was built in the midst of his city, at the point where the two main thoroughfares crossed each other. Encased in a translucent sarcophagus, it stood there for centuries, for all to see.

After Alexander's death his generals carved up the Greek world between them. It had been rumored that Ptolemy was Alexander's half-brother, and that his mother was a mistress of Phillip II who, having got her pregnant, had her married off to one of the obscure courtiers by the name of Lagus. Ptolemy was certainly as clever as he was ambitious. Within a year of his arrival in

Alexandria, he had extended his power over Cyrene, one of the oldest Hellenic colonies on the Libyan seacoast. In the end, he followed the lead of the other Macedonian generals and proclaimed himself king. He now ruled over Egypt as Ptolemy Soter, the Savior (305–285 BC).

Ptolemy proceeded to adorn his new capital with architecture and scholarship. He began building a massive lighthouse on the little island of Pharos that stood in the middle of the harbor and a dyke to connect it with the mainland, the heptastadion. The beacon of the lighthouse extended some fifty miles out to sea, guiding Greek ships to the port of Alexandria. Ptolemy also founded the Library and the Mouseion, institutions designed to promote Hellenic learning and scholarship. He was himself a literary man and an author of a history of Alexander's campaigns, much admired by later historians. To run the Mouseion, he imported Demetrius of Phalerum, a well-known scholar and statesman who had governed Athens for ten years on behalf of Cassander. Demetrius became Ptolemy's consultant on religious and cultural affairs. He planned the Mouseion along the lines of its Athenian predecessor that contained the library of Aristotle.

In collaboration with Manetho, a native Egyptian priest of Ra in Heliopolis, Demetrius conceived a new god for the Ptolemaic kingdom: Sarapis. The statue of Sarapis, ascribed to the Greek sculptor Bryaxis, showed him seated in Greek garments upon a classic throne. His countenance was that of Zeus or Pluto though somewhat softened and more benign. The basket on his head showed that he was a harvest god, while the three-headed Cerberus at his feet (the Greek Anubis) indicated that he was also a god of the underworld. The cult of Sarapis was housed at Rakotis, the native heart of the city. Everything in Alexandria, from its streets to its patron god, was thought out and carefully designed in advance.

Not that the Ptolemies were so foolish as to admit this. The legend was put about and later recorded by Plutarch that Ptolemy Soter had seen a colossal statue in a dream, though he had previously neither known nor seen it. In the dream the statue ordered him to have it transported to Alexandria as quickly as possible. When he explained the vision to his friends, a much-traveled man was found who said that he had seen such a statue in Sinope in Greece. After some difficulty and with the help of divine intervention the statue was stolen and brought to Alexandria. It was Manetho and Timotheus, the interpreter, who had convinced Ptolemy that the statue represented none other than Sarapis.[1]

Ptolemy had commissioned Manetho to write the history of Egypt, known to posterity as the *Aegyptiaca*. For the Museion, he recruited Euclid, author of a textbook on geometry that remained standard all the way down to the twentieth century. It was Euclid who told Ptolemy that there was no royal road to geometry and that this subject was equally demanding even of kings. Another learned recruit was Heraphilus of Chalcedon (ca. 330–260 BC), an anatomist specializing in the brain and the nervous system.

Although the precise date of the Mouseion's founding is uncertain, we know that it was well established, together with the accompanying library, by 285 BC. That year, the 82-year-old Ptolemy decided to share power with his favorite son, also called Ptolemy, deliberately overlooking an older son by an earlier marriage, a move opposed by Heraphilus. As a punishment, Ptolemy II had him exiled to Upper Egypt, where he was said eventually to have committed suicide with an asp. The prestige of the Mouseion, however, was confirmed when in 270 BC the scientist Strato of Lampsacus was called from Athens to be director. Some classical writers recorded that Strato brought with him Aristotle's library, which was purchased by Ptolemy II.

The library was of great importance as the repository of the written word. Backed by royal patronage, it quickly outgrew its Athenian predecessor. In time, it had accumulated more than 700,000 volumes and had become the largest library of its time. The post of librarian held great prestige. The directors of the library included Eratosthenes of Cyrene (ca. 276–195 BC), the first geographer to calculate the circumference of the globe (correct to within fifty miles of modern measurements), and Aristarchus of Samothrace (217–145 BC), the celebrated grammarian and literary critic.

By the time the architect Sostratus completed the Pharos lighthouse in the rule of Ptolemy II (285–246 BC), Alexandria had become the beacon of the civilized world. Ptolemy II Philadelphus ("Friend of his Sister") was the first to invite the Jews to settle and trade. He also saw the advantage of having good relations with Rome and by the close of the third century BC the Romans were trading with Egypt and aiding her politically.

The second Ptolemy was best known for marrying his sister Arsinoe in 277 BC. She was seven years older and when they married he already had a wife. Although this was anathema to Greek sensibilities, he had a prototype in Egypt and cited the myth of Osiris and Isis as his sacerdotal justification. He and Arsinoe were deified and venerated as the "Dioscuri," also claiming descent from Zeus. Like their Egyptian predecessors who practiced incest, the Ptolemies had once again managed to "keep the business in the family by keeping the family in the business."[2]

Their successors followed the custom of self-deification and were often represented with Egyptian and Greek divine attributes. Ptolemy II established a four-yearly festival called the Ptolemaia, intended to honor his father and the dynasty he founded. He had wanted it to rival the Olympic Games. Callixeinus of Rhodes described the "pompe" or procession of Dionysus performed in the city's stadium and the remarkable pavilion constructed in the palace for the great "symposion" or drinking party. Above the door of the pavilion flew the flag with the Ptolemaic eagle flanked by Dionysus and Apollo.

Deification of rulers may have been common enough in Egypt, but the Greeks could not accept it in all seriousness. Plutarch summed up the Greek attitude thus:

> If certain men, elated with arrogance and inflamed mentally with youthful folly and pride accepted divine names and the building of temples to them, this reputation blossomed for only a short time. Then, after incurring also the charge of vanity and ostentation together with impiety and lawlessness, *transient, they rose like smoke in air and flew away* . . . That is why the old man Antigonus said, when a certain Hermodotus addressed him in a poem as "son of Helios" and "god," "*My chamber-pot carrier doesn't see these qualities in me!*"[3]

Ptolemy III Eugertes, Well-doer (246–221 BC), was the son of Ptolemy II by his first wife. He was a soldier with a taste for science who married his cousin Berenice of Cyrene in Libya, thereby securing Cyrene, which had lapsed, back for the Ptolemaic kingdom. Berenice was the most praised of all the Ptolemaic queens and had a constellation named after her hair, which had fallen out. During their reign, the power of Alexandria achieved its greatest height. The tomb of Alexander had become famed in the Hellenic world and the Ptolemaic kings and queens had themselves buried close to it. A theatre and a racecourse were built near the palace and the temple of Sarapis was completed in the Greek style. Neither the tomb of Alexander nor the Ptolemaic tombs have yet been discovered. The layout of the Greek city, drowned by the invading sea and buried under layers of all the subsequent cities that were to follow, still eludes archaeologists.

Judging by descriptions, the Greek city was the product of a single scheme, laid down by Dinocrates and completed by the first three Ptolemies. It was beautiful, but as E. M. Forster pointed out: "It exhibited all the advantages and perhaps some of the drawbacks of a town that had been carefully planned. There was a majesty of all the considered effects; but there also may have been a little dullness . . . the place was more Greek than Greece . . . brand new, gleaming white, a calculated marvel of marble."[4]

After the death of Ptolemy III the dynasty declined. Ptolemy IV hardly ever left the palace and people did not know for a year that he had died. The fury of the Alexandrian mob when they discovered that they had been uninformed about the death of their king showed itself in the lynching of his minister Agathocles. "The savagery of the Egyptians is truly appalling when their passions are aroused," wrote Polybius. Murder and civil war raised instability in the kingdom to a disastrous level. A long conflict between Ptolemy VI and

VIII frequently involved the interventions of the mob. When the portly Ptolemy VII came puffing along the harbor to greet the envoy of the Roman Senate, the latter said: "At all events the Alexandrians have seen their king walk."

The dynasty was well known for its ambitious queens. Arsinoe III faced the Syrian army at Rafa and Cleopatra III had murdered her own son. Against this background rose the stern figure of Rome. It first intervened in Egyptian affairs in 168 BC, halting the invasion of the Seleucid king Antiochus. Polybius wrote that on this occasion the Senate's ambassador treated the Seleucid king in a manner that was "peremptory and exceedingly arrogant." He took a stick, drew a circle round Antiochus and commanded him to decide to leave Egypt before crossing the line. Antiochus, who had lived in Rome and assessed her might, complied. After that, Rome had more power in Egypt than the Ptolemies, but saw no need to exercise it. Only when the struggles of the first century BC shook up the Roman republic did Egypt come to play a part in Rome's affairs.

In 80 BC, the Alexandrian mob had assassinated their own king, Ptolemy X. In the aftermath, the Roman dictator Sulla installed Ptolemy XI on the throne. In 60 BC the first triumvirate was forged between Caesar, Pompey, and Crassus. In 49 BC Pompey became guardian of Ptolemy XIII, the "Flute Player." After the death of Ptolemy XIII, his daughter Cleopatra VII assumed the throne jointly with her younger brother, not yet of age. Pompey deposed her. The dissolution of the triumvirate in Rome led to civil war. Caesar defeated Pompey at Pharsalus in 48 BC, went to Egypt, reinstalled Cleopatra on the throne, and spent two months with her, fathering a son, Ptolemy Caesarion. Six years later, after Caesar's assassination, Cleopatra became the lover of Mark Anthony, one of the members of the second triumvirate, forged in the aftermath of Caesar's death. Anthony fathered three of Cleopatra's children. His Egyptian escapades made it easy for Octavian, Caesar's nephew and another triumvir, to smear his reputation, declare war, and defeat him at the battle of Actium in 31 BC. Octavian's victory led to the suicides of Anthony and Cleopatra and the Roman capture of Alexandria.

Despite this long political decline, the intellectual eminence of Alexandria was acknowledged by all. The earlier cultural achievement, especially Greek, was recognized and preserved for future generations. Literary, philosophic, and religious texts were collected, systematically examined, and painstakingly edited. Humanistic scholarship was founded. New disciplines were developed and analyses and commentaries produced. Education itself had become systematized and widespread. Schools, gymnasia, and theatres were plentiful and instruction in Greek philosophy, literature, and rhetoric available.

When Julius Caesar wanted a new calendar, he commissioned an Alexandrian astronomer. The original Egyptian version still survives in the Coptic calendar today, while the somewhat revised Roman calendar was used in Europe until 1582, in England and America until 1752, and in Russia until 1919. Caesar also wanted to map out the fountains of the Nile, mentioned by Herodotus. The Roman historian Lucan, the nephew of Seneca, wrote that Caesar was put off by a long and unclear story about the Nile's course and length by the priest Acoreus. The Nile, said the priest, rose on the equator in the tropic of Cancer and meandered through forest and desert until reaching Egypt at Philae. This account did not satisfy Caesar, who was looking for a pathway through Africa. He had asked for a map and had got a myth.[5] The sources of the Nile remained elusive until the nineteenth century.

Literary activity in Alexandria was not limited to the Greek community. By 100 BC, the standard Greek translation of the Old Testament, known as the Septuagint, was produced by scholars drawn from the extensive Jewish population. Hebrew had long been displaced in importance as a living language and the Septuagint was created for the use of the Greek-speaking Jews of Alexandria, Cyrene, and Asia Minor. The Septuagint, meaning "seventy" in Latin, had given rise to the legend that the translation was done by seventy wise men working simultaneously. At the very least, the translation probably kept busy several generations of diligent scholars. It is more likely that the name Septuagint referred to the approval given to the Greek version for non-ritual use by the Sanhedrin, the body of seventy-one priests, scribes, and elders who were both the supreme court of justice and the highest governing council for the Alexandrian Jews. A single copy of the Septuagint remains the most ancient complete version of the Old Testament known to us. It was the Septuagint that was quoted in the New Testament. The earliest Christians, including the apostles, probably read it, and it is still used by the Greek Orthodox Church today.

Notwithstanding this great wave of new intellectual creativity, the Ptolemies also made a dedicated effort to uphold Egyptian religious traditions. They built the temples of Hathor at Dendera, Horus at Edfu, Sobek at Kom Ombo, and Isis at Philae. The latter was built at one of the many sites claiming to contain the tombs of Osiris and Isis. Seneca in the first century AD wrote about "the veins of the Nile" at Philae where the inundation was first observed. He also reiterated the belief that the Nile could cure barren women.

At Dendera, the chapel of Osiris was built with a dome over it, decorated with the image of the zodiac. While preserving the prehistoric star religion of Egypt and its association with Osiris, the zodiac was essentially a late Hellenized mixture of Egyptian and Babylonian symbols.

The marriage between the Greek and Egyptian sensibilities was less than perfect. From the days of Herodotus on, the Greeks had perceived Egypt as a somewhat outmoded, exotic wonderland on the Nile. The Ptolemies capitalized on this romanticized, oriental dazzle for their own political ends. Their temple endowments kept the priesthood happy and projected their "popular" image. But they looked out on the Mediterranean rather than toward the Nile valley. The vital forces of the time came from the Hellenized world. Outside Alexandria, Egypt was gradually turning into a cultural backwater.

Ptolemaic art exhibits a curious amalgamation of styles. In Upper Egypt, the Egyptian canon was adhered to but the impact of Greek art had brought noticeable changes to the old style. The Greek inclination toward naturalism and movement when applied to the Egyptian canon diluted the strength of its iconic, formulaic shapes. In Alexandria, Greek artists made little more than a playful use of misunderstood Egyptian motifs.

The Egyptian of the Ptolemaic era was exposed to a multiplicity of influences and viewpoints. One gets the feeling that although temple rituals and festivals were maintained, the old ways were being fast forgotten. Greek graffiti written below the painted reliefs illustrating the Books of the Afterlife in the tomb of Ramses VI reveal bewilderment about their meaning: "I, Dioscorammon, saw this folly and it puzzled me"; "Epiphanius declares he saw nothing to admire but the stone."[6]

At the temple of Dendera, a new ritual of Osiris marked the final development of the cult. It was of such importance that the king officiated at the performance, attended by gods and goddesses of the land who were present in the form of statues. Forty-two priests from the forty-two districts of Egypt formed a procession. Each held a canopic jar with one of the remnants of Osiris's body. The jars held the contribution of the respective district to the reconstitution of Osiris. The procession, headed by the king, went up to the roof of the temple where the contents of the forty-two vessels were poured together inside a gilded sycamore chest, as the king recited the following words:

> I bring you the capitals of the districts
> they are your limbs,
> they are your *ka* which is with you,
> I bring you your name,
> your *ba*, your shadow, your form, your image, and the towns of your districts.
> I bring you the main gods of Lower Egypt joined together.
> All the members of your body, they are united.[7]

Egypt was seen as the body of Osiris, the forty-two districts as his limbs. The embalming ritual was applied to the whole land to heal its disintegration, to unite, inspirit, and renew it. It was as if the country tried to hold on to its collective memory to avert the threat of national amnesia. The Egyptian world had come apart, its power spent in the process of diffusion. The old myths were dying.

In the cosmopolitan culture of Alexandria, Greeks and Egyptians lived side by side. It had not occurred to them that one religion was false and another true. Each worshiped their own gods and spoke their own language, but never thought that the gods of their neighbors had no existence. The Greeks, for one, were willing to believe that the Egyptian gods were probably their own gods under a different name. Osiris was Sarapis, Dyonisus, and Adonis; he had become their own hero.

Among the many poets on the payrolls of Ptolemy II and Ptolemy III was Theocritus, a Sicilian by birth. Theocritus' best-known works were his Idylls, "little pictures" that pulled together a number of Hellenic trends to create the beginning of a new genre: "pastoral" poetry. The idyll Women at the Festival described the Alexandrian outing of two lady friends, Praxinoe and Gorgo. Through chariots, crowds of people, "big boots and men in soldiers' cloaks," the ladies made their way to the palace of Queen Arsinoe, where a famous singer performed at the yearly festival of Adonis.

The celebration had all the hallmarks of an Egyptian festival. The life-size image of the god was laid out in the middle of a great hall and in front of it the singer sang a hymn of praise. The only difference was that he sang in Greek and that the image of the dying and resurrected god of Egypt had acquired the blond curls and rosy cheeks of a Greek youth.

CHAPTER 11

THE ROMAN LEGACY

If one decided to look at the land of Egypt as the body of Osiris, like the priests of Dendera had done, then Egypt's long history could be read as the biography of the god. Osiris had emerged from the mists of prehistory in Nubia, floated down the Nile and absorbed virtually all the other cults at one time or another, and survived the advent and dismantling of monotheism and all the foreign invasions. The ideas of sacrifice, faith as the food of life, and the resurrection of the soul were archetypal and lived on through all the religious and cultural changes.

When Christianity arrived in Roman Alexandria the Egyptians had been long prepared. Osiris was as alive in Byzantine Alexandria as he had been in prehistoric Nubia. One can easily imagine him smiling as an Easter procession passed carrying icons of the bearded savior, seeing himself set off into the future as Christ Arisen. Isis would have been by his side, the savior-child in her arms, while a boat waited to carry them across the sea to Greece and the birth of modern Europe.

The thought of ancient Egypt, sifted through the cosmopolitan culture of Alexandria, had found its way into the future. Although Alexandria had become no more than a provincial capital after the Roman conquest, her philosophy thrived. All three groups of her citizens – Egyptians, Greeks, and Jews – gave a significant contribution to the new religions and philosophies that sprang up around the turn of the era.

The Romans had continued to worship Sarapis. It was probably through the Romans that his religion had spread among the Slavs who lived on the edges of the Black Sea. In the Russian language the verb *ozaritsya* – to become "Osirified" – means simultaneously "to die" and "to become enlightened." In this double meaning are found Egyptian doctrines of the New Kingdom.

In the Roman world the most popular of the Egyptian deities was Isis. Her cult had spread steadily from the fourth century BC on and temples to her had

111

been built all over the empire (including France and the British Isles). In Rome she was worshiped as *Regina victrix* who bestowed victory over death on her followers. As Isis-Sirius she was the guarantor of the Nile inundation and the fertility of Egypt and Rome. Her ancient significance for the Egyptian calendar was reflected in her role as mistress of the New Year.

The Platonic philosopher Lucius Apuleius described how Isis had revealed herself to him in a dream:

> All the perfumes of Arabia floated into my nostrils as the heavenly voice of this great goddess deigned to address me – You see me here, Lucius, moved by your prayer. I am Nature, the Universal Mother, mistress of all the elements, primordial child of time, sovereign of all things spiritual, Queen of the Dead, first among the immortals, the single manifestation of all gods and goddesses that are.

The initiation ritual into the mysteries of Isis, as described by Apuleius in Book 11 of the Metamorphoses, also contained traces of the ancient religion. Breaking the professed secrecy of initiation, Apuleius described how the initiate experienced a symbolic death, after which he confronted the gods and goddesses and passed through the four elements of earth, water, fire, and air. The height of the mystery was the appearance of the sun at midnight, which conveyed to the dazzled devotee the certainty of overcoming death.

This episode was reminiscent of the journey of Ra through the netherworld, described in the Books of the Afterlife. It was at midnight that the sun united with Osiris and completed his renewal. Then, light was borne "on the arms of darkness." In scene 73 of the Book of Gates the souls gazed directly at the face of the sun, sharing in the certainty of eternal life. In the Egyptian religion this glimpse was possible only after crossing the threshold of death; it was a matter of constantly renewed regeneration. For Apuleius, it was a release from the forces of fate and mortality.

Apuleius also described the effigy of Osiris in the shape of an urn of burnished gold with a long spout on one side and a handle on the other. While he praised the urn as "worthy of devotion because of its skillful craftsmanship and originality," he proclaimed that its contents were "ineffable . . . [and] should be veiled in deep silence." On the island of Delos Osiris was worshiped as Hydreios, the personification of the sacred Nile vessel.

From Augustus on, imperial patronage for scholars had become available only in Rome. Leonidas of Alexandria, an astrologer and a poet, moved permanently to Rome in the middle of the first century of the Christian era, where he was patronized by no less than three emperors. Philo, an Alexandrian Jewish philosopher described with amusement his unsuccessful visit to Rome in AD 40 as head of a delegation to the mad emperor Caligula. Philo had attempted to defend the right of the Jews to have their own religion. "Are you the infidels who do not worship me as a god?" Caligula asked with indignation. Philo almost got himself and the delegation killed, but using the emperor's momentary distraction he signaled to his company to quietly slip out of the room.

At this time, the Wisdom of Solomon was written and eventually included in the Apocrypha. The author was unknown, but he was a Jew who wrote in Greek and had studied Stoic and Epicurean philosophy as well as the Egyptian rites. This could be accomplished only in Alexandria. He introduced Sophia or Wisdom as the intermediary between the god of the Old Testament and his people: "She is more beautiful than the sun and all the order of stars: being compared with light, she is found beyond it." The similarity of Sophia to Isis also points to an Egyptian inspiration. In Christianity, the role of Sophia was taken over by Mary.

In Philo, the Jewish school of Alexandria reached its height. In his writings, Philo, an orthodox Jew, tried to reconcile Judaism with Greek philosophy. Philo developed the idea that god created the world through his Logos or Word. The Word was the outward expression of god's existence. Philo may have made a link to the Egyptian idea that a word had a literal, magic presence as substance rather than representation. Although he made the shift from magic to philosophy, he had at his disposal an underlying tradition going back for thousands of years. "Those who can see," wrote Philo, "lift their eyes to heaven, and contemplate the Manna, the divine Word. Those who cannot see, look at the onions on the ground."

"By Logos, the whole world is now become Athens and Greece," wrote Clement of Alexandria. Not only was the Old Testament read in Greek, but also Greek philosophy had succeeded in becoming an indelible part of the Jewish faith. The ideas of Philo may have influenced the Gospel of St. John.

Also around the turn of the era, or shortly thereafter, was written the Corpus Hermeticum, eighteen books in Greek and one in Latin – Asclepius. The Hermetic books were religious and philosophical writings attributed to Hermes Trismegistus – three times great. In contrast to the rational Philo, they explored the mystic tradition stemming from the ancient magic of Thoth. The correspondence of Hermes with Thoth, who was qualified by the triple adjective "great," was affirmed already in the original texts.

It is in the Coffin Texts of the Middle Kingdom that we first hear of a divine book of Thoth. In this historical period, the tradition of Thoth as the author of sacred writings, wisdom, and magic was inaugurated. Thoth was the scribe at the judgment of Osiris. His nature evolved still further in the New Kingdom, when he became credited with all invention. Sacred writings were ascribed to him or said to be found at the feet of his statue. He played an important part in a number of spells from the Book of the Dead, where he was given the task of registering the passengers in the boat of the sun, as they "disembark and embark."

In the Late Period, Thoth had become the overall master of magic. Magical spells written by him (often with invisible ink) were considered especially effective. Love charms and healing spells were the most popular. Thoth also wrote letters of introduction for the dead to smooth their way through the underworld, and, together with Isis, he was credited with having composed the Books of Breathing. Cicero wrote that the Egyptians were reluctant to speak his name, so strongly was his magic feared. The oft-repeated legend about the forty-two sacred books of Thoth was probably related to the forty-two districts of Egypt and the totality of the Egyptian tradition. In Egyptian art Thoth was represented as an ibis or a baboon.

In the Hermetic writings, Thoth-Hermes had acquired a human image. It has been suggested that this was due to his identification with Imhotep-Asclepius by the Greeks.[1] The books of the Corpus Hermeticum were written in the form of dialogues between Hermes and his son Tat or between Hermes and his disciple Asclepius. There were also dialogues between Isis and Horus in the book entitled Kore Cosmou – Virgin of the World. The Egyptian mystical approach to deity was perhaps best expressed in the Hermetic definition of Isis: "I am all that is, was and will be and no mortal has ever lifted my veil." Centuries later, the German philosopher Emmanuel Kant wrote that this was the loftiest sentiment ever voiced.

No single binding Hermetic doctrine was taught in the books, except that knowledge was obtained through revelation rather than reason. Tractate XVI of the Corpus even attacked the "verbal din" of Greek philosophy. According to Kore Cosmou, the gods had endowed the priests of Egypt with three arts: philosophy and magic for the soul and medicine for the body. The Hermetic aim was to obtain the secret lore that had once been revealed by the ancient masters.

"The essence of all is One," said the Hermetic texts. From the Oneness of the original being came the law of correspondence between all the planes or spheres of existence, in virtue of which the macrocosm was the same as the microcosm, the universal as the individual, the world as human and the human as god. "An earthly man," it was said in The Key, "is a mortal god and the heavenly god is immortal man." There was no savior, nor was there a battle between good and evil. All being modes of the One, no inherent antagonism or essential difference was possible. Unconsciousness was non-being; it was as darkness opposed to light. Just as light was a positive entity, darkness was a non-entity. Hermetism avoided anthropomorphism by defining divinity itself to be neither life, nor mind, nor substance, but the cause of these.

Hermetism was a religion without temple or cult. It simply extolled the wisdom preserved in the Egyptian temples. Indeed, the Hermetic writings were permeated by Egyptian religious teaching. The idea of the hidden universal god as One and All was developed in the New Kingdom. Hermetism advanced in the Egyptian temples of late antiquity, where learned people continued to cultivate the worship of Imhotep as Asclepius in the attempt to preserve the religious ideas of ancient Egypt.

Towards the end of the second century two new intellectual phenomena emerged in Alexandria: Neoplatonism and Christianity. The Neoplatonic school was founded by Ammonius Saccas, a man who had begun his life as a Christian and a porter in the docks of Alexandria. He abandoned both for the study of Plato. Though nothing is known of his teachings, he produced great students: Longinus, Origen, and Plotinus.

All three had exalted careers, but Plotinus became the most famous of all. He was born in Assyut about 205. He did not like to talk about the date and place of his birth, considering the day his soul descended into his body to be a great misfortune. After completing his training in Alexandria, he joined a military expedition against Persia in order to learn about Persian and Indian philosophy. In the process, he nearly lost his life, saved himself by flight, and the following year he retired to Rome, where he began to teach philosophy. He had numerous followers, plebeians as well as emperors, and was greatly admired for his honesty and candor. After his death, his pupil Porphyry collected his notes and published them in nine volumes called the Enneads.

Plotinus' god had three grades: he was a trinity. From him emanated all creation and he was the goal to whom all things strive to return. The whole universe had an inclination towards good and we were all parts of god even if we didn't realize it. People were inherently divine and in order to achieve their full potential, rebirth was allowed them. Glimpses of god were attainable through the mystic vision, since god was our true self.

> The Fatherland is there whence we have come, and there is the Father . . . This is not a journey for the feet . . . you must close your eyes and call instead upon another vision which is to be waked within you . . . Withdraw into yourself and look . . . when you are self-gathered into the purity of your being, nothing now remains that can shatter that inner unity . . . Now call up all your confidence, strike forward yet a step – you need a guide no longer – forward yet a step – you need a guide no longer – strain and see.
>
> This is the only eye that sees the mighty Beauty . . . To any vision must be brought an eye adapted to what is to be seen, and having some resemblance to it. Never did the eye see the sun unless it had first become sun-like, and never can the soul have a vision of the first Beauty unless itself be beautiful.[2]

Plotinus' Egyptian roots were unmistakable, but he went one step further and offered a bridge between the Mystic Vision and rational philosophy. His difference with the Egyptian faith lay in his belief in reincarnation and in his inspired vision of the awakened, fulfilled man as god. It has been suggested that he talked with Hindu merchants on the quays of Alexandria – he came nearer than any other philosopher did to the thought of the East. The ideas of Plotinus were to play a pivotal role in the rise of Christianity, particularly in the writings of Paul and Augustine.

Simmering through the Jewish communities, the Christian religion reached Egypt as early as the first century. According to the Egyptian Church, Christianity was introduced to Alexandria by St. Mark, who was martyred in 62 for protesting against the worship of Sarapis. On its arrival, Christianity encountered the spiritual life of ancient Egypt that had clung to the soul of the Nile valley for over four thousand years. It had existed so long, that it was impossible to uproot it from the hearts of the people. The partaking of Osiris as the food of life, the judgment of the soul in the next world, and the resurrection of Osiris as the risen sun had sunk deeply into the minds of the people. So had baptism in the sacred river, wearing black as a sign of mourning god's sacrifice, and sprinkling the faithful with Nile water. Isis had been called "the mother of god" centuries before Mary. The birth of the savior-child at the winter solstice is still celebrated by the entire Christian world.

Did Christianity take from the Osiris myth the doctrines of resurrection, the immortality of the soul, and the sacrament of the Eucharist? It is more certain that much of its symbolism was used in popular art. Isis and Horus became the Virgin and Child, Horus and Seth became St. George and the Dragon. The church of St. George in Coptic Cairo was built on the site of an earlier temple dedicated to the immortal battle between Horus and Seth. Eventually, St. George came to be venerated as the patron saint of Cairo. In early Christian tombs, the Christian cross and the ankh symbol of Isis were often depicted side by side. Egyptian symbols were simply adapted to the new faith.

When Christianity reached Alexandria, the new religion of the poor folk of Palestine underwent a philosophic blossoming. The link between people and god, the Logos of Philo and the Emanations of Plotinus, had become manifest in Christ. Christ, too, was the divine emanation that issued from the Father, the Word, and the Way. His human incarnation, his redemption of the world through suffering, were all familiar. "Thus, Christianity did not burst upon Egypt as a clap of thunder, but stole into ears already prepared," Forster wrote.[3]

Christian orthodoxy was advocated by Clement, head of the theological college in Alexandria. In trying to recommend Christianity to a cosmopolitan and philosophically inclined audience, Clement did not denounce Judaism or

Greek philosophy. He taught that they were all preparations for the Gospel of Christ. Philosophy had prepared the Greeks, just as the Jewish Law had prepared the Jews. The Greek sense of time was cyclical, like the Egyptian. The Judaic was linear and progressive, the gradual fulfillment in time of God's plan for man. The fusion of these divergent traditions with the Gospel of Christ was possible only in the intellectual climate of Alexandria.

Among the teachings of Roman Alexandria flourished Gnosis or secret knowledge. The Gnostics believed that creation was a flaw, the work of an inferior deity or Demiurge who wrongly believed himself to be god. Christ was sent to counteract the ignorance of the Demiurge and establish the link to the divine. Gnosis was essentially dualistic Christianity that maintained the ancient notions of opposites as complementary forces. Gnosis also employed magical spells and mystical writings with numbers and letters that touched on the world of ancient Egyptian magical texts. Emphasis was laid on secret knowledge through which, in the Egyptian tradition, salvation and redemption could be achieved. "I know, therefore I am pure," proclaimed the souls in the Book of the Dead.

The Gnostic god Abraxas appeared on magical gems as a human figure with the head of a rooster and feet shaped like serpents. In the tomb of Ramses VI the sun god was represented with serpent feet. Abraxas, called a "fearsome god" by Carl Jung, was also a solar god, identical to the supreme deity Iao, the Old Testament Yahweh.[4] The numerical value of the Greek letters of his name, 365, also identified him with time.

With Constantine (306–37) Christianity became the official religion of Rome and the Byzantine Period began. The future of the empire now looked to the east, to the new Rome. Although paganism was not extinguished among the Egyptians, most of the population had become Christian before the end of the fourth century.

Alexandria, with its schools and libraries and rich spiritual life, shared in the triumph of Christianity. The bishop of Alexandria soon took on the title of Patriarch and began appointing other bishops for Egypt and Ethiopia. He is still the nominal head of the Ethiopian Church. The Egyptian Church dated its founding not from the birth of Christ, but from the "Era of the Martyrs" (284), proudly commemorating its own contribution to the triumph of faith.

However, Alexandria's hopes of playing a predominant role in the Christian world were quickly shattered. In Constantine's lifetime Arius and Athanasius, both native Alexandrians, clashed in their definitions of the nature of Christ. Was he of the same or the like substance as the Father? The subtlety of their argument, as well as the deep convictions held by both, soon confounded all Christian thinkers. Constantine, a pragmatist and no theologian himself, was appalled by the schism that rapidly divided his empire. It seemed a wise solution to accept one view as true and condemn the other as heresy. This was accomplished amid violent disputes at the Council of Nicaea on the Black Sea in 325, attended by 250 bishops and many priests. Athanasius had won the argument, but the battle was not over.

In the centuries that followed two more controversial doctrines on the nature of Christ sprung up in Alexandria: Monophysm and Monothelism. Monophysm upheld the doctrine of the Single Nature of Christ. In Christian orthodoxy, Christ was believed to have a two-fold nature because he was the Son of God as well as the son of Mary. Monothelism affirmed the Single Will of Christ, as opposed to the orthodox definition of the two wills of Christ: the human and the divine that operate in unison. Monophysm was championed by the Patriarch Dioscuros, the founder of the Coptic Church, and is still upheld by the Ethiopian Church. Monothelism remains the creed of the Maronites in Syria to this day.

In Alexandria itself, the age of hatred and misery was fast approaching. After the triumph of Athanasius, the Patriarchate had become all-powerful. Although in theory Egypt belonged to the Byzantine emperor, who sent a prefect and an army garrison from Constantinople, in practice the Patriarch and his army of monks ruled it. By the fourth century the monks had gathered into formidable communities from which they made raids on the city. They were hostile to its pagan heritage and averse to its culture. After Christianity had been made compulsory at the end of the fourth century, the monks attacked the worship of Sarapis. The god's temple at Canopus was destroyed in 389, the parent temple at Alexandria two years later. With it disappeared the famous library, its books stored in the cloisters around the building.

The cloak of religion hid nationalist passions. The very name of the Church – "Coptic" – meant Egyptian; its official language was Egyptian. Though written with Greek letters (with six additions, adapted from hieroglyphs), the Greek language was rejected, the ancient one revived. Racial trouble, averted by the Ptolemies and the Romans, at last broke out. It divided Egyptian society and paved the way for the Arab conquest. Greeks were no longer safe in Egypt, particularly educated Greeks.

It was at this time that knowledge of the location of Alexander's tomb and the tombs of the Ptolemaic kings and queens was lost. The persecution of the pagans continued and culminated in the killing of Hypatia in 415. She was the daughter of Theon, director of the Platonic school, and had succeeded her father at the academy. She was a Greek, a pagan philosopher, and an educated woman. None of these things was acceptable any more and she was torn apart by the wild, black-robed army of monks, "human only in their faces." With her cruel, public murder, the Hellenic spirit of Alexandria expired forever.

The cult of Isis, one of the last bastions of paganism, came to an end after Theodosius (379–95) forbade the pagan cults in 391, the same year that the Serapeum of Alexandria was pillaged and closed. But as late as the fifth century we hear of the existence of pagan temples in Egypt and of an Isis festival celebrated by peasants in north Italy. At the beginning of the sixth century, the statue of Isis from the temple at Philae was still carried up the Nile to Sudan to bless the crops. Although the temple was officially closed down in the middle of the sixth century, medieval historians wrote that as late as the tenth century, people from local villages still gathered at Philae for the annual feast of Isis. It is from Philae that we have the last hieroglyphic inscriptions.

EPILOGUE

Every new world springs from an older one.
Greek proverb

In the year 250, near Heracleus in Upper Egypt, Anthony the Abbot was born. He began his religious life living in an ancient tomb near his village on the Nile. There, he wrestled with snakes, demons, and lurid visions that may have looked at him from the walls. Having mastered these temptations, Anthony left the world behind, walked into the wilderness, and retired by a spring of water in the hills of the eastern desert. His admirers became so many that he was persuaded to build shelters for them and to give them the rules of life. These were the first monasteries. His followers were the first monks. Anthony was venerated as a living saint in his own lifetime. The emperor Constantine wrote to him and asked to be remembered in his prayers. Patriarch Athanasius paid him many visits and wrote the account of his life. Monasticism, rooted in the Egyptian desert, came to play an important part in the religious life of medieval Europe.

Though it fiercely rejected anything pagan, the early church was deeply indebted to ancient Egypt. The vivid pictures of the Egyptian afterlife, the fiery hell and the fields of peace, resonated in Christian texts. The descent of Jesus into the underworld became part of the Christian iconography after the fourth century – Christ had become the sun in the realm of the dead. In the Gnostic text Pistis Sophia, sins were punished in the outer darkness, represented as a twelve-limbed ouroboros dragon, and the dungeons of punishment were guarded by animal-headed demons.

In the fifth century, the Coptic abbot Shenouda wrote the following: "Even if your eyes are put out, you will rise up again with your eyes at the resurrection . . . Even if your head is cut off, you will rise up with it . . . the little finger of your hand will not be missing, nor the little toe of your foot." The idea of the perfect, immaculate body rising to eternal life came from the ancient religion. Now, it was retold in the legends of the Coptic martyrs.

It took some time for the doctrines of the official church to prevail over popular beliefs and customs. Mummification continued in Christian circles and it was only Islam that brought it to an abrupt end. On mummy covers, Christian symbols were used together with images of the ancient gods. We are told that Carpocrates, a second-century philosopher in Alexandria, "having secretly made icons of Jesus and Paul and Pythagoras and Homer, in their honor burnt incense and worshiped them."

Devotion to the lion god Bes was especially tenacious. Amulets with Bes were buried in Coptic graves and in a Coptic papyrus Bes was equated with Christ. His oracle at Abydos was still popular around AD 500 and until the twentieth century the inhabitants of Karnak told lively stories about a Bes-like spirit who danced at night in the ruins of the temple.

Many legends grew around the stay of the Holy Family in Egypt. It is still widely believed that they spent three and a half years in the monastery of Deir-el-Muharraq, 40 miles north of Assyut. In the winter of 2001–2 miraculous lights were said to illuminate the church and thousands of pilgrims flocked to see them. The route of the Holy Family was said to proceed through Matareya, where a sacred tree is still worshiped in their honor. Another popular legend described how the holy family spent the night in the forecourt of the temple of Thoth-Hermes, where the idols shattered noisily while prostrating themselves before the young Christ.

The new religion absorbed the old. In 641 the Arab armies conquered Egypt. The Egyptians adopted the Arabic language, the majority the Islamic faith, though a part of the people remained Christian in spite of a tax levied on them by the Arabs. The Coptic Church of Egypt still has some 6 million followers. As their homeland became part of the larger Arab world, the Egyptians, blessed by the Nile, went on farming and fishing and living in the shadows of their ancient temples.

The cult of Osiris, subsumed as it was by Sarapis, was defeated by the new monotheistic religions. Or was it? The so-called Gnostic gospels (early Christian texts) found hidden in a jar in the Upper Egyptian village of Nag el Hamadi, contained Gnostic texts as well as fragments from Asclepius. Many of the early Church Fathers remained interested in Hermetic philosophy. Augustine, who had a Gnostic and Manichean past, dedicated several chapters of his City of God to Hermes Trismegistus. He often quoted from Asclepius, including the passage where Egypt was called "the temple of the world." But he objected to the worship of statues, mentioned in the book. Augustine considered Hermes to be a "wise man" and a precursor of Christianity.

121

The apostle Paul, following Hermetic teaching, wrote that to be spiritual was the precondition of all spiritual knowledge. Only insofar as one developed one's consciousness could one become the organon of knowledge, capable of obtaining truth. Thus, from being "agnostic" and incapable of knowledge, one ought to become "gnostic" – to know oneself and god and to become aware of the substantial identity of the two.

Alchemical texts appeared in the Arabic language as early as the eight century. Some of them were ascribed to the Ummayad prince Khaled. In Arabic writing alchemy was often described as the "wisdom of the temples." It is now believed that the Emerald Tablet, reputed to have been discovered in the tomb of Hermes under his statue, was the work of an Arab alchemist of the eighth or ninth century. It was said to contain the heart of Hermetic philosophy.

A Medieval Arab manuscript entitled the Great Circular Letter of the Spheres quoted the myth of Osiris as its inspiration. The "letter" was said to have come from an inscription concealed under a statue of Artemis (Isis-Hathor) in the crypt of the temple at Dendera. It had been translated from Greek into Arabic at the time when Caliph Ma'amun stayed in Egypt in 832. It described a king in the process of decaying who engendered an heir in whom he will live again. The Nile inundation was compared to quicksilver, aqua vitae. In the same "letter," references were made to a text called Isis the Prophetess to her Son Horus and the celebration of the New Year's festival at the beginning of the inundation in Egypt was mentioned.

The third-century philosopher Zosimus of Panopolis (modern Akhmim), who was widely quoted in the Arab texts, referred to the alchemical process as "Osirification." The fifth-century historian Olympiodorus of Alexandria wrote that the tomb of Osiris was the image of alchemy. A frequent metaphor used in the alchemical texts referred to the divine chest with enigmatic contents, the knowledge of which only the magician possessed. It seems more than likely that this was the chest of Osiris, his earth-body.

In antiquity, Jewish tradition viewed Moses as an Egyptian and often equated him with Hermes. Manetho, Strabo, and Tacitus also considered Moses an Egyptian. In Acts 7.22 it was said that he was "educated in the wisdom of the Egyptians." Philo wrote that he was initiated into the "symbolic" philosophy of Egypt and that he was the inventor of writing and philosophy. Just as Thoth carried his writing tablet, so Moses carried the tablets of the Ten Commandments – he was the first in the Old Testament to make use of writing. By the eighth century, Cosmas, the bishop of Jerusalem, viewed Moses and Hermes as contemporaries who were initiated together into Egyptian wisdom, thus rejecting the claim that they were identical. The dispute about the Egyptian origins of Moses still continues.

Gnostic ideas also lived on, in spite of the Christian persecution. Through-out the Middle Ages in Europe, Gnosis provided a kind of subculture. It was followed by the Bogomils ("those who are dear to god"), who spread from Bulgaria to Bosnia and Dalmatia. In the Balkans, Gnostic groups disappeared only after the arrival of Turkish rule in the fourteenth century.

In the eleventh century, Gnostic groups appeared in Germany and northern Italy. The Cathari, a religious movement that adhered to Gnostic dualistic notions, remained active throughout the twelfth century. In southern France, the movement was supported by the nobility and was defeated only after prolonged struggles. The first Crusade against them took place in 1209 and another in 1255.

The Latin translation of the Arab alchemical texts appeared in Europe as early as 1144. They were translated by the same author who also translated the Qu'ran. From then on, alchemy became part of the Western tradition as well. During the Renaissance the Hermetic writings inspired renewed interest. By then, they were regarded as the work of a single author. In 1460 Leonardo of Pistoia brought them from Macedonia to the Platonic Academy in Florence. This institution was founded at the court of the Medici to resume the legacy of the Athenian Academy, closed by Justinian in 529. Marsilio Ficino translated the Greek texts into Latin at the bequest of Cosimo de Medici. They were held as evidence that philosophy existed even before Plato. Ficino's book underwent sixteen printings before the end of the sixteenth century. The Neoplatonic corpus, studied at the Florentine Academy, implied the existence of a universal religion of which Christianity was perhaps the ultimate, but not the only, manifestation.

The Latin translation of the Emerald Tablet was first published in 1541. From Latin it was translated into many European languages. The Emerald Tablet does indeed appear to be indebted to the ancient Egyptian religion. The correspondence of the stars with the elements, the exaltation of the sun, the union of the heaven of Ra and the underworld of Osiris, the New Kingdom doctrine of god as One and All, the pluralistic trinity – all are there:

> In truth, certainty and without doubt,
> whatever is below is like that which is above,
> and whatever is above is like that which is below,
> to accomplish the miracles of one thing.
>
> And just as all things proceed from the One,
> meditated by the One, so all things
> are born from this one thing by adaptation.

123

Its father is the Sun
its mother is the Moon.
The Wind carries it in its belly.
Its nurse is the Earth.

It is the father of every miraculous work
in the whole world. Its power is perfect
if it is converted into earth.
Separate the earth from the fire
and the subtle from the gross,
softly and with great prudence.

Ascend from earth to heaven,
and descend again from heaven to earth,
and unite together the power
of things superior and inferior.

In this way you will acquire the glory of the whole world
and all darkness will leave you.
This is the power of all powers,
for it conquers everything subtle
and penetrates everything solid.

Thus is the world created. From this,
and in this way, wonders are made.

For this reason I am called Hermes Trismegistus, for I possess
the three parts of wisdom of the whole world.

Perfect is what I have said
of the works of the sun.

The last two lines relate the Emerald Tablet quite literally to the solar religion of Heliopolis. At the end of the seventeenth century no less a personage that Sir Isaac Newton composed a commentary on the natural philosophy expounded in the Emerald Tablet. His manuscript is kept in the Cambridge Library. From the Renaissance on there had been a peculiar collaboration between science and the esoteric tradition. Newton had also studied alchemy at considerable length.

Hermetism had its opponents, too. In 1614 Isaac Casaubon wrote that the Corpus was a fake created by the early Christians. Francis Bacon also renounced Hermes in his Platonically inspired utopian work New Atlantis and acknowledged only Moses as a lawgiver. But all those who longed to be freed from the straitjacket of ecclesiastical dogma saw in hermetism a mode of alternative thinking. It played a part even in politics. Egypt was presented either as a positive model of a strong, enlightened monarchy or a negative model of oppression and priestly rule. Both views were used as critiques of their own day and age. Revolutionaries, Rosicrucians, Freemasons, and other societies – secret and public – drew their inspiration from it.

Napoleon's expedition to Egypt in 1798 may have been inspired by this cultural climate. Taking forty thousand soldiers with him, Napoleon went to lift the veil of Isis and suffered a military disaster. However, the hundred artists and scholars who accompanied the army won a cultural victory. The artist Denon, assigned to General Desaix's division, described arriving in Thebes: "This forsaken city . . . so haunted our imagination, that at the sight of these scattered ruins the army came to a halt of its own accord and spontaneously began to applaud, as if occupying the ruins of this capital had been the purpose of this glorious enterprise, thus completing the conquest of Egypt."[1]

In 1802, Denon published his *Voyage dans la Basse et la Haute Egypte pendant les campagnes du General Bonaparte*. Napoleon's scholars published four additional volumes entitled *Description de l'Egypte publiee sous les ordres de Napoleon Bonaparte* in 1822. Egyptian art became more widely known in Europe and in the same year of 1822 Champollion deciphered the hieroglyphic script, having studied new, hitherto unknown texts. Champollion and those who followed him expanded the knowledge of Egypt, freeing themselves from classical and biblical interpretations. With the rise of science in every sphere of thought a more sweeping dismissal was given to the esoteric elements of the ancient tradition.

However, a surge of Egyptomania had been propelled. Napoleon's Egyptian campaign, the raising of obelisks in various European capitals, and the opening of the Suez Canal, had all caught the public attention. Egyptian art with its forever-young gods and goddesses, kings and queens, and its bucolic scenes of daily life appeared as if it communicated some golden age of human happiness. People fell in love with Egypt as if with their own fabled past. The romantic image of Egypt flourished; it had molded itself to the art of the day and remained relatively unaffected by developments in Egyptology.

The story of Osiris continued to live in the Hermetic tradition. In the English edition of the Virgin of the World and Asclepius, published in London in 1885, Edward Maitland, who wrote the introduction, gave his own interpretation of the mystic Osiris, Egyptian kingship, and the judgment in the netherworld: "Osiris is the reflection and counterpart in man of the supreme lord of the universe, the ideal type of humanity. Hence, the soul, or essential ego, presenting itself for judgment in the spiritual world, is described as an Osiris. It is to this Osiris or king within us, our higher reason, the true world of god, that we owe perpetual reverence, service and faithful allegiance."[2]

Moreover, Maitland had taken on board Darwin's theory of evolution, for he explains the Hermetic teachings in the context of evolutionary principles:

> The Hermetic books admit three expressions of deity: first, the supreme, abstract and infinite god, eternally self-subsistent and unmanifest; secondly, the only-begotten, the manifestation of deity in the universe; thirdly, god in man, the Redeemer or Osiris . . . The microcosmic Sun or Osiris, was the image and correspondence of this macrocosmic Sun; the regenerating principle within man, begotten by the means of the soul's experience in Time and Generation . . . Isis is thus the secret motive-power of Evolution; Osiris is the ultimate ideal of Humanity toward the realization of which that Evolution moves.[3]

Hermetism, ancient mythology, and the mystery religions have been reemerging to play new roles on the current intellectual scene. The evocative power of Egypt is constantly being enhanced by new interpretations. Hermetism's universal appeal led to a new publication of Hermetica in 1992. Hermetic symbols are still widely used – none more so than the eye in the pyramid, the symbol of Osiris reborn, that ended up on the American dollar bill. The all-seeing eye is likely to have made its way to America with the Rosicrucians and the Freemasons. This image was first used on the capstone of the pyramid of Khendjer, who ruled during the seventeenth century BC. It is almost four thousand years old. On the opposite side to the pyramid on the dollar bill the American eagle holds a scroll with the inscription *e pluribus unum*: "One from Many."

Today, in the world of clashing religions and belief-systems, perhaps the most important bequest of the ancient religion is found in its pluralism, its accommodative spirit, the happy coexistence of the One and the Many, and the faith in the indivisibility of all created things. The ancient gods appear almost as secular, invisible gods. Their humanity, travails, errors, and acts of reparation reveal a world of genuine tolerance. Hence their adaptability to the dynamic changes of the world. The Osiris archetype provided so strong a metaphor that it has come down to us today, if only as a faint echo, through a multiplicity of traditions. Their first seed can perhaps be found in the black Nilotic mud of prehistoric Egypt.

Plutarch, who gave us the myth of Osiris and Isis, thought that it immortalized above all people's eternal quest for knowledge and beauty.

Whenever [the souls] are freed and pass over to the formless, invisible, dispassionate, and holy kingdom, then is this god their leader and king, for depending on him, they behold insatiably and desire the beauty which is, to men, ineffable and unutterable. This beauty, as the ancient story shows, Isis ever loves and she pursues it and unites with it, filling this our world with all the beautiful and good qualities which have a part in creation.[4]

NOTES

1 The Myth Makers

1 Herodotus, book II, chapter 19; see G. Rawlinson, *Herodotus: The Histories* (London, 1997).

2 Pliny, *Historia Naturalis*, book 5, chapter 58; see I. Shaw, *The Oxford History of Ancient Egypt* (Oxford, 2002), p. 428.

3 Plutarch, 72; see J. G. Griffiths, *Plutarch: De Iside et Osiride* (Oxford, 1970).

4 E. Baumgartel, *Cultures of Prehistoric Egypt* (Oxford, 1947); A. Roberts, *Hathor Rising: The Serpent Power of Ancient Egypt* (Wiltshire, 1995); A. Roberts, *My Heart, My Mother: Death and Rebirth in Ancient Egypt* (Sussex, 2000).

5 For the description of the prehistoric stone circle arranged to mark the rising of Sirius in the Western Desert of Egypt, see F. Wendorf and J. McKim Melville, "The Megalithic Alignments" in F. Wendorf, R. Schild, and Associates, *Holocene Settlement of the Egyptian Sahara, Vol. 1: The Archaeology of Nabta Playa* (London, 2001), pp. 489–502; and J. McKim Melville et al., "The Calendar Circle," *Nature* 392 (April 1998), pp. 488–92.

6 C. G. Seligman, *Pagan Tribes of the Nilotic Sudan* (London, 1932); and C. G. Seligman, "The Cult of the Nyakang and the Divine Kings of the Shilluk," in *Fourth Report of the Welcome Tropical Research Laboratories at the Gordon Memorial College*, vol. B (Khartoum, 1911), pp. 221–5. In 1998 the Sudanese state television aired a documentary about the ritual burial of the aged Shillouk king still practiced by this southern tribe. Women from the royal harem announced the time when the king's powers began to fail and it was then that his sacrifice was effected. His willing burial ensured that the spirit of the First Ancestor passed on into the new king.

7 M. Rice, *The Making of Egypt: The Origins of Ancient Egypt from 5000–2000 BC* (London, 1991), p. 34. This theory is disputed by some prehistoric scholars who see the late prehistoric period as "evolution rather than a sudden break." See I. Shaw (ed.), *The Oxford History of Ancient Egypt* (Oxford, 2000), p. 53.

3 Abydos

1 G. Dreyer, *Umm el-Qab. Nachuntersuchungen im fruehzeitlichen Koenigsfriedhof*, 3./4. Vorbericht. *MDAIK* 46 (Mainz, 1990), pp. 76–8.

2 In New Kingdom inscriptions in the temple of Karnak it was said that *neheh*, one of the two pillars of eternity that supported the sky, would fall and the earth would then be flooded by the waters "as at its beginning, and neither god nor goddess will remain." However, Osiris and Atum would survive in the primeval ocean Noun, ensuring the potential renewal of the cycle of *neheh*. Although the threat was permanently present, nothing was ever definitively lost. See C. Traunecker, *The Gods of Egypt* (Ithaca, NY, 2001), pp. 37–9.

3 Herodotus, book II, chapter 86; see G. Rawlinson, *Herodotus: The Histories* (London, 1997).

4 Pyramid Builders

1 Plutarch, 29; see J. G. Griffiths, *Plutarch: De Iside et Osiride* (Oxford, 1970).

2 Most scholars estimate the number of stone blocks in the Great Pyramid to have been 2.3 million. In an article in *KMT: A Modern Journal of Ancient Egypt*, 13, 3 (Fall, 2002), A. Sakovich claims the number was as high as 3.617 million.

3 Herodotus, book II, chapter 124; see G. Rawlinson, *Herodotus: The Histories* (London, 1997).

4 Gustave Flaubert, *Flaubert in Egypt*, trans. F. Steegmuller (London, 1996), p. 50.

5 Herodotus, II, 124.

6 M. Lichtheim, *Ancient Egyptian Literature* (London, 1973), vol. 1, pp. 3–7.

7 J. Allen, "Reading a Pyramid," in *Hommages a Jean Leclant v. 1, Etudes Pharaoniques* (Cairo: Institut Francais d'Archeologie Orientale, 1994), pp. 5–28; and J. Allen, "The Cosmology of the Pyramid Texts," *Yale Egyptological Studies* 3 (New Haven, CT, 1989), pp. 89–101.

8 A. Piankoff, *The Tomb of Ramesses VI* (New York, 1954), p. 51; also see E. Hornung, *The One and the Many: Idea into Image* (Princeton, NJ, 1992).

9 R. H. Frayar, ed., *The Hermetic Works: The Virgin of the World of Hermes Mercurius Trismegistus* (London, 1885), p. 139.

10 Assar or Ashur in both Babylonian and Hebrew means "gracious." See J. G. Griffiths, *The Origins of Osiris and his Cult: Studies in the History of Religion* (Leiden 1980), p. 91; also S. Smith, "The Relation of Marduk, Ashur and Osiris," *Journal of Egyptian Archaeology* 8 (1922), pp. 41–4.

11 E. W. Lane, *An Account of the Manners and Customs of the Modern Egyptians Written in Egypt during the Years 1833–1835* (London, 1989), pp. 483–4.

12 Herodotus, II, 62.

13 R. E. Witt, *Isis in the Ancient World* (Baltimore, MD, 1997), p. 92.

14 Plutarch, 36.

15 Plutarch, 65.

5 The Mysteries

1 Herodotus, book II, chapter 69; see G. Rawlinson, *Herodotus: The Histories* (London, 1997).
2 Herodotus, II, 90.
3 E. W. Lane, *Description of Egypt* (Cairo, 2000), p. 444.
4 Herodotus, II, 149.
5 See I. Shaw, ed., *The Oxford History of Ancient Egypt* (Oxford, 2000), p. 166.
6 Herodotus, II, 148.
7 Both Maspero and Lichtheim describe this work as satirical; Helck, on the other hand, has denied its satirical tone and humorous content. For its justification as a satire, see M. Lichtheim, *Ancient Egyptian Literature* (London, 1973), vol. 1, p. 184.
8 E. Hornung, *The Secret Lore of Egypt* (Ithaca, NY, 2001), p. 5.
9 Lichtheim, *Ancient Egyptian Literature*, vol. 2, p. 84.
10 Plutarch, 28; see J. G. Griffiths, *Plutarch: De Iside et Osiride* (Oxford, 1970).
11 Plutarch, 20.
12 R. E. Witt, *Isis in the Ancient World* (Baltimore, MD, 1997), p. 162.
13 The precise dating of the month presents some difficulties. The great procession under the direction of Ikernofret occurred on the 22nd of Thoth (July), according to the festival calendar. On the other hand, Plutarch recorded that Athyr (September) was the month of the festival. Calendar texts of Ramesses III and of the Ptolemaic temple at Dendera mention the month of Khoiak (November). Under Augustus, the date was the 28th of Mesore (June). The discrepancy between these records may be explained by the moving, rotating dates of festivals, calculated within the system of lunar months and the rising of the stars. The dating of the Muslim feast of Ramadan moves eleven days every year in order to conform to the lunar dating system. The fitting of old Egyptian lunar dates into solar calendars, many of which were adopted hundreds of years later, may have led to different calculations of the precise month. We know from Plutarch that the burial of Osiris took place in autumn, before the plowing season. The festival of Abydos, whenever it took place, would have hearkened back to ancient Djedu and the sacrificial rites of plowing.
14 Plutarch, 39. The preparing of the chest of Osiris is also described on the Dendera inscriptions; see E. Otto, *Egyptian Art and the Cults of Osiris and Amon* (London, 1968), p. 60, fig. 5. The chest of Osiris furnished the model for the corn mummies of the Late Period.
15 According to the Dendera calendar.
16 Otto, *Egyptian Art*, pp. 42–3.
17 Lichtheim, *Ancient Egyptian Literature*, vol. 1, p. 124.
18 Plutarch, 54.

6 Rise of the Empire

1 Passage in Josephus in which he claims to be quoting directly from Manetho; see I. Shaw (ed.), *The Oxford History of Ancient Egypt* (Oxford, 2000), p. 195.
2 From the Kamose Stelae; see Shaw, *Oxford History*.
3 The previous Dynasty Fourteen consisted of minor rulers who ruled contemporaneously with the kings of Dynasties Thirteen and Fifteen.
4 The forensic examination of the mummy of Kamose, now in the Egyptian Museum in Cairo, indicates that the king was kneeling on the ground when a fatal blow was delivered to his head.
5 Shaw, *Oxford History*, p. 238.
6 Herodotus, book II, chapter 47; see G. Rawlinson, *Herodotus: The Histories* (London, 1997).

7 Golden Pharaohs

1 M. Lichtheim, *Ancient Egyptian Literature* (London, 1973), vol. 2, pp. 96–100.
2 Some scholars believe that the queen who wrote the letter was Nefertiti. See C. Aldred, *Akhenaten, King of Egypt* (London, 1988); on the possible role played by Nefertiti in the late Amarna period, see J. Harris, "Neferneferuaten," in *Goettinger Miszellen* 4 (1973), pp. 15–17; also J. Tyldesley, *Nefertiti, Egypt's Sun Queen* (London, 1998).
3 See Aldred, *Akhenaten*.
4 See J. Assmann, *Egyptian Solar Religion in the New Kingdom* (New York, 1995).
5 R. Krauss, "Amenmesses," *Studien zur Altaegyptischer Kultur* 24 (1997), pp. 161–84, identifies the name of this king with that of the biblical Moses.
6 E. Wente, "A Letter of Complaint to the Vizier To," *Journal of Near Eastern Studies* 20 (1961), pp. 252–7.
7 H. Goedicke, "Was Magic used in the Harem Conspiracy against Ramses III?" *Journal of Egyptian Archaeology* 49 (1963), pp. 71–92.
8 Since both the name and face of the king on the sarcophagus were erased and destroyed in antiquity in an act of *damnatio memoriae*, it is not clear who the king was. However, the magical sun-dried clay bricks placed as protection for the tomb were inscribed with Akhenaton's name. Other objects found in the tomb belonged to Akhenaton's immediate family.

8 Books of the Afterlife

1 J. Bishop, *Joyce's Book of the Dark: Finnegans Wake* (Madison, WI, 1986), pp. 99–104.
2 See A. Piankoff, *The Shrines of Tutankhamun* (New York, 1955).

3   In the Egyptian language the grammatical plural could also have the dual form.
4   Plutarch, 36; see J. G. Griffiths, *Plutarch: De Iside et Osiride* (Oxford, 1970).
5   R. H. Frayar, ed., *The Hermetic Works: The Virgin of the World of Hermes Mercurius Trismegistus* (London, 1885), p. 71.

9 Toward the Sunset

1   Translation of Wiedemann's text quoted from S. Schama, *Landscape and Memory* (London, 1996), p. 256.
2   Plutarch, 20; see J. G. Griffiths, *Plutarch: De Iside et Osiride* (Oxford, 1970).
3   Plutarch, 16.
4   Herodotus, book II, chapter 177; see G. Rawlinson, *Herodotus: The Histories* (London, 1997).
5   Diodorus, I, 83, 8; see *Diodorus of Sicily*, trans. C. H. Oldfather, London, 1933.
6   Herodotus, II, 60.
7   Plutarch, 11.
8   Cyril of Alexandria, *In Isaiam*, II, iii; see J. P. Migne, *Patrologia Graeca* (Paris, 1856–7), vol. 70, p. 441.

10 Greeks in Egypt

1   Plutarch, 28; see J. G. Griffiths, *Plutarch: De Iside et Osiride* (Oxford, 1970).
2   F. E. Adcock, *Greek and Macedonian Kingship* (London 1953), p. 171.
3   Plutarch, 24.
4   E. M. Forster, *Alexandria: A History and a Guide* (New York, 1961), p. 23.
5   S. Schama, *Landscape and Memory* (London, 1996), p. 262.
6   Greek graffiti in the tomb of Ramses VI translated by A. Piankoff, *The Tomb of Ramesses VI* (New York, 1954), p. 3.
7   J. Assmann, *The Mind of Egypt* (New York, 2002), p. 109.

11 The Roman Legacy

1   E. Hornung, *The Secret Lore of Egypt: Its Impact on the West* (Ithaca, NY, 2001), pp. 48–55.
2   E. M. Forster, *Alexandria: A History and a Guide* (New York, 1961), pp. 71–2.
3   Forster, *Alexandria*, p. 75.
4   Yahweh, originally "YHWH," had been variously translated as "I am who I am," "I am that I am," "He brings into existence whatever exists," and "I am/shall be who I am/shall be," where the complex ambiguity between the present and the future tense is unresolved. The meaning of the word remains controversial.

Epilogue

1 *Egyptomania: Egypt in Western Art 1730–1930*. Exhibition catalogue (Canada, 1994), p. 202.
2 R. H. Frayar, ed., *The Hermetic Works: The Virgin of the World of Hermes Mercurius Trismegistus* (London, 1885), p. 113.
3 Frayar, *The Hermetic Works*, p. xxx.
4 Plutarch, 78; see J. G. Griffiths, *Plutarch: De Iside et Osiride* (Oxford, 1970).

GLOSSARY

Adonis   "The Lord"; the god of Phoenicia.

Akh   One of the three parts of the soul, the enlightened spirit which after death lived among the imperishable stars of the northern sky.

Amduat   The book of "what is in the netherworld"; a New Kingdom literary composition.

Ankh   The hieroglyphic sign of life.

Apuleius   Platonic philosopher of the second century AD, born at Madaura in north Africa. He studied at Carthage, Athens, and Rome. His most famous work is the Golden Ass, written in eleven books; the description of the initiation into the Mysteries of Isis was described in the volume entitled the Metamorphoses.

Assar   "The good god"; Ashur in Babylonian and Hebrew.

Astarte   Phoenician goddess of love; her name was derived from the Mesopotamian Ishtar.

Ba, ba-bird   One of three parts of the soul, the soaring breath of life, sometimes represented as a bird with a human head and arms.

Ba'al   The supreme god of Syria, Phoenicia, and Cana'an. His consort was Ashera, a version of Ishtar or Astarte.

bark, bark-shrine   Sacred boat used to carry divine images.

Book of the Dead   Funerary writings known to the Egyptians as the "spell of stepping forth into daylight."

cataracts of the Nile   Six rapids or rocky areas between Assuan and Khartoum which made the Nile difficult to navigate.

Coffin Texts   A group of over a thousand spells written on coffins of the Middle Kingdom.

Diodorus of Sicily   Nicknamed Siculus. The only information about his life and work can be found in his own Library of History. He was born in Agyrium in Sicily (he does not mention the date of his birth) and traveled

134

to Egypt in the year of the eighteenth Olympiad (57–56 BC). The task he set himself was to compose a universal world history, from the creation to his own day. Of the forty books he wrote, only fifteen are extant.

Dionysus   Greek god of wine, revelry, ecstasy, and chtonic powers (the Roman Bacchus). Dionysiac processions involved carrying phallic images, hence Herodotus identified Osiris with Dionysus.

Divine Consort of Amun   A religious title held by women, attested in the Eighteenth Dynasty; it became closely associated with "God's Wife," who played the part of the consort of Amun in religious ceremonies at Thebes. From the Twentieth Dynasty on the lady who held the title, usually the king's daughter, was required to remain celibate and to adopt her successor from among the royal family.

Djed-pillar   Amulet of Osiris in the form of stalks tied into a stack.

Djedu   A town in the Delta, the first attested cult center of Osiris. The Greek Busiris (modern Abusir).

Duat   The netherworld, written with the star symbol, the world of night, where the gods lived.

Faience   Non-clay ceramic material used to make jewelry, amulets, and vessels. It was usually glazed to have a shiny turquoise color.

false door   A carved image of a door in stone or wood usually found in tombs, a symbolic threshold to the next world.

Herodotus   Called "the father of history" by Cicero. Born in Halicarnasus (modern Bodrum) in 484 BC, he traveled to Egypt and Italy, collecting all the information he could obtain about the history and origin of nations. His Histories covered a period of about 240 years, from Cyrus the Great to Xerxes of Persia. Herodotus publicly recited his Histories to the people assembled at the Olympic games (guided by a considerable desire for fame, as his contemporaries noted) and was always received with universal applause. His work was esteemed so highly by his contemporaries that the names of the nine muses were given to the nine books of which it was composed and he enjoyed a lasting celebrity throughout all the Greek states.

hieroglyphs   Greek *hieros glyphos* – "sacred carvings." The name of the traditional Egyptian script that consisted of ideograms and phonograms, written both horizontally and vertically, left to right or right to left, used from the late prehistoric period to the fourth century AD.

Hierophant   Greek for sacred priest.

Hittites   The Egyptian Hatti, an Indo-Aryan people whose kingdom was in Anatolia, with the capital in Hattushash (modern Bogazkoy).

Horus name   The first royal name in the sequence of names which made up the Egyptian royal titulary.

Hyksos   Greek version of the Egyptian *hekau khasut*, rulers of foreign (literally, mountainous) countries.

Hypostyle hall   Greek for "bearing pillars"; a temple court filled with pillars, lit up by clerestory windows in the roof.

Instruction   A type of literary text consisting of aphorisms and ethical advice.

Ishtar   Mesopotamian goddess of love and war.

Ka   One of the three elements of the soul, the shadow, the double, the vital power by which one lived during life and after death.

Kush   The kingdom in Sudan with the capital of Napata (modern Karima), situated in the area of the fourth cataract of the Nile.

Labyrinth   The temple of Amenemhat III in the Fayoum oasis.

Litany of Ra   A literary composition of the New Kingdom that exalted the sun-god.

Mamisi   "Birth house," a term invented by Champollion to describe a building in the temples of the Late and Ptolemaic Periods in which the marriage of the goddess (Isis or Hathor) and the birth of the divine child were celebrated. It was usually placed at right angles to the main temple axis.

Mittani   A kingdom situated between Allalakh and Carchemish in Syria. It played a prominent part in Egyptian foreign relations, particularly during the reigns of Amenhotep III, Akhenaton, and Tutankhamun. The Mittani were of Aryan descent.

mummy   Egyptian *sah*, an embalmed corpse wrapped in bandages.

necropolis   Greek for "city of the dead."

Nilometer   A kind of well used to measure the flood rise of the Nile, usually consisting of steps marked with cubit measurements.

obelisk   a tall, square column with a pyramid top, sacred to the sun-god.

Opening the Mouth ceremony   A funerary ritual in which a mummy or a statue was infused with life (i.e., the mouth was "opened" and the image "breathed").

Orion   Egyptian *sah*, a constellation in the sky associated with Osiris.

ostracon   Greek for "potsherd"; fragments of pottery or limestone flakes used for writing letters and drawing sketches.

ouroboros   A snake biting its own tail, the Egyptian "tail-in-mouth."

Plutarch   A philosopher and writer born in AD 44 in Chaeronea, near Delphi in Greece. He traveled around Greece and Egypt and opened a school in Rome. He may have left Rome in the aftermath of Domitian's expulsions of philosophers from the city, returning to the peaceful and solitary retreat of his native town "to cling . . . lest it become smaller." Plutarch taught philosophy in Chaeronea and Athens (of which he was also a citizen) and served as priest in the temple of Delphi. He produced an enormous amount of work of which we possess perhaps half. It was in

Delphi that he wrote the chronicle entitled On Isis and Osiris. It was dedicated to Clea, a priestess of Isis.

Punt   An African kingdom from whence the Egyptians imported myrrh, hardwood, ivory, and other African goods. Thought to have been located in southern Sudan, Somalia, or the Eritrean coast of Ethiopia.

Pyramid Texts   A collection of 759 chapters of funerary texts; the earliest religious writings in Egypt, written on the walls of the pyramids of the late Old Kingdom.

Sarapeum   The temple of Sarapis in Alexandria; also the underground vaults used for the burial of the Apis bulls in Memphis.

Satrapy   A province in the Persian empire.

Scarab   The sacred scarab beetle (*scarabaeus sacer*) used as a symbol in writing and to designate Khepri, the rising sun, a manifestation of the solar trinity.

Sed festival   A royal jubilee of renewal and regeneration.

Sem priest   "Son of the god" who performed the ancestor ritual; a Sem priest also officiated at the Opening the Mouth ceremony during the king's funeral.

Sirius   Egyptian *sopdet*, brightest of the fixed stars, related to Isis.

Soma   The mausoleum of Alexander the Great in Alexandria.

sphinx   A mythical beast with a human head and lion body, usually representing the king or queen. Sometimes sphinxes were given ram heads or hawk heads.

Strabo   A geographer born at Amasia in Pontus. He composed his Geography in the fourth year of the emperor Tiberius.

Suetonius   A Roman historian of the first century AD, secretary to Hadrian; his most famous work is the Twelve Caesars.

Sumer, Sumerians   *Shu-mer* (black heads); people of southern Mesopotamia who developed one of the earliest cultures of the Near East in the fourth millennium BC.

triad   A group of three gods, usually a divine family.

tyet   An amulet of Isis in the form of a ribbon tied to resemble the ankh sign of life.

udjat   An amulet of Horus in the form of an eye. It was said to represent the wounded eye of Horus restored by the sun-god. Worn to ward off evil influences.

Viceroy of Kush   The Egyptian official governing Nubia and Kush, a title established in the New Kingdom.

Zeus   Supreme god of the Greek pantheon.

EGYPTIAN CHRONOLOGY

Early Dynastic	**ca. 3000–2686 BC**
First Dynasty	ca. 3000–2890
Narmer	
Aha	
Djer	
Djet	
Den	
Queen Merneith (regent)	
Anedjib	
Semerkhet	
Qa'a	
Second Dynasty	2890–2686
Hetepsekhemwy	
Raneb	
Nynetjer	
Weneg	
Sened	
Peribsen	
Kasekhemwy	
Old Kingdom	**2686–2160 BC**
Third Dynasty	2686–2613
Nebka	2686–2667
Djoser	2667–2648
Sekhemkhet	2648–2640
Khaba	2640–2637

Sanakht?	
Huni	2637–2613
Fourth Dynasty	2613–2494
Snofru	2613–2589
Khufu (Cheops)	2589–2566
Djedefra	2566–2558
Khafra (Chephren)	2558–2532
Menkaura(Mycerinus)	2532–2503
Shepseskaf	2503–2498
Fifth Dynasty	2494–2345
Userkaf	2494–2487
Sahura	2487–2475
Neferirkara	2475–2455
Shepseskara	2455–2448
Raneferef	2448–2445
Nyuserra	2445–2421
Menkauhor	2421–2414
Djedkara	2414–2375
Unas	2375–2345
Sixth Dynasty	2345–2181
Teti	2345–2323
Userkara (a usurper)	2323–2321
Pepy I	2321–2287
Merenra	2287–2278
Pepy II	2278–2184
Nitokret	2184–2181

Seventh and Eighth Dynasties
Interregnum

First Intermediate Period	**2160–2055** BC

Ninth and Tenth Dynasties (Heracleopolis)	*2160–2125*

Khety (Merybra)
Khety (Nebkaura)
Khety (Wahkara)
Merykara

Eleventh Dynasty (Thebes only)	2125–2055
Mentuhotep I	
Intef I	2125–2112
Intef II	2112–2063
Intef III	2063–2055

Middle Kingdom	**2055–1650** BC
Eleventh Dynasty (all Egypt)	2055–1985
Mentuhotep II	2055–2004
Mentuhotep III	2004–1992
Mentuhotep IV	1992–1985

Twelfth Dynasty	1985–1773
Amenemhat I	1985–1956
Senusret I	1956–1911
Amenemhat II	1911–1877
Senusret II	1877–1870
Senusret III (Sesostris)	1870–1831
Amenemhat III	1831–1786
Amenemhat IV	1786–1777
Queen Sobek-neferu	1777–1773

Thirteenth Dynasty	1773–after 1650

Wegaf
Sobekhotep II
Neferhotep
Ameny-intef-amenemhat
Hor (Awibra)
Khendjer
Sobekhotep III
Neferhotep I
Sa-hathor
Sobekhotep V
Ay

Fourteenth Dynasty	1773–1650

Minor rulers contemporary with
Dynasties Thirteen and Fifteen

Second Intermediate Period	**1650–1550** BC

Fifteenth Dynasty (Hyksos)

Salitis	
Khyan	ca. 1600
Apepi	ca. 1555
Khamudi	

Sixteenth Dynasty	1650–1580

Theban rulers contemporary
with the Fifteenth Dynasty

Seventeenth Dynasty	ca. 1580–1550 BC

Rahotep
Sobekemsaf I
Intef VI
Intef VII
Intef VIII
Sobekemsaf II
Siamun

Ta'a (Seqenenra)	ca. 1560
Kamose	1555–1550

New Kingdom	**1550–1069** BC

Eighteenth Dynasty	1550–1295
Ahmose	1550–1525
Amenhotep I	1525–1504

Thutmose I	1504–1492	Amenemnisu	1043–1039
Thutmose II	1492–1479	Psusennes I	1039–991
Thutmose III	1479–1425	Pinnodjem (Thebes)	
Hatshepsut	1473–1458	Amenemope	993–984
Amenhotep II	1427–1400	Osorkon (the Elder)	984–978
Thutmose IV	1400–1390	Siamun	978–959
Amenhotep III	1390–1352	Psusennes II	959–945
Amenhotep IV/			
Akhenaton	1352–1336	*Twenty-second Dynasty*	945–715
Smenkara	1338–1336	Sheshonq I	945–924
Tutankhamun	1336–1327	Osorkon I	924–889
Ay	1327–1323	Sheshonq II	ca. 890
Horemhab	1323–1295	Takelot I	889–874
		Osorkon II	874–850
Ramessid Period	**1295–**	Takelot II	850–825
	1069 BC	Sheshonq III	825–773
Nineteenth Dynasty	1295–1186	Pimay	773–767
Ramses I	1295–1294	Sheshonq IV	767–730
Sety I	1294–1279	Osorkon IV	730–715
Ramses II	1279–1213		
Merenptah	1213–1203	*Twenty-third Dynasty*	818–715
Amenmesses	1203–	Six kings contemporaneous with	
	1200?	the Twenty-second Dynasty	
Sety II	1200–1194		
Siptah	1194–1188	*Twenty-fourth Dynasty*	730–715 BC
Queen Tausert	1188–1186	Tefnakht	
		Bakenrenef (Bocchoris)	720–715
Twentieth Dynasty	1186–1069		
Setnakht	1186–1184	*Twenty-fifth Dynasty*	747–656
Ramses III	1184–1153	Piy	747–716
Ramses IV	1153–1147	Shabaqo	716–702
Ramses V	1147–1143	Shebitqo	702–690
Ramses VI	1143–1136	Taharqo	690–664
Ramses VII	1136–1129	Tanwetamani	664–656
Ramses VIII	1129–1126		
Ramses IX	1126–1108	**Late Period**	**664–332 BC**
Ramses X	1108–1099	*Twenty-sixth Dynasty*	664–525
Ramses XI	1099–1069	Nekau I	672–664
		Psamtek I	664–610
Third Intermediate	**1069–664 BC**	Nekau II	610–595
Period		Psamtek II	595–589
Twenty-first Dynasty	1069–945	Apries	589–570
Smendes	1069–1043	Amasis	570–526
Herihor (Thebes)		Psamtek III	526–525

Twenty-seventh Dynasty	525–404		
(Persian)			
Cambyses	525–522		
Darius I	522–486		
Xerxes I	486–465		
Artaxerxes I	465–424		
Darius II	424–405		
Artaxerxes II	405–359		
Twenty-eighth Dynasty	404–399		
Amyrtaios	404–399		
Twenty-ninth Dynasty	399–380		
Nepherites I	399–393		
Hakor	393–380		
Nepherites II	ca. 380		
Thirtieth Dynasty	380–343		
Nectanebo I	380–362		
Teos	362–360		
Nectanebo	360–343		
Second Persian Period	343–332		
Artaxerxes III (Ochus)	343–338		
Arses	338–336		
Darius III	336–332		

Ptolemaic Period   **332–30 BC**

Macedonian Dynasty	332–305
Alexander the Great	332–323
Phillip Arrhidaeus	323–317
Alexander IV (nominal ruler)	317–310
Ptolemaic Dynasty	305–30
Ptolemy I Soter	305–285
Ptolemy II Philadelphos	285–246
Ptolemy III Eugertes	246–221
Ptolemy IV Philopator	221–205
Ptolemy V Epiphanes	205–180
Ptolemy VI Philometor	180–145
Ptolemy VII Neos Philopator	145
Ptolemy VIII Eugertes II	170–116
Ptolemy IX Soter II	116–107
Ptolemy X Alexander I	107–88
Ptolemy IX Soter II (restored)	88–80
Ptolemy XI Alexander II	80
Ptolemy XII Neos Dyonisus	80–51
Cleopatra VII Philopator	51–30
Ptolemy XIII	51–47
Ptolemy XIV	47–44
Ptolemy XV Caesarion	44–30

Roman Period   **30 BC–AD 395**

Egypt was officially established as a Roman province on August 31, 30 BC. Christianity was instituted by Constantine I (AD 306–37) and all pagan cults outlawed by Theodosius in 391. The Roman empire was divided into western and eastern parts in 395. The Byzantine Period is designated as Coptic in Egypt.

BIBLIOGRAPHY

Adcock, F. E. *Greek and Macedonian Kingship*, London, 1953.

Aldred, C. *Akhenaten and Nefertiti*, New York, 1973.

—— *Akhenaten, King of Egypt*, London, 1988.

J. Allen, "The Cosmology of the Pyramid Texts," *Yale Egyptological Studies* 3, 1989, 89–101.

—— "Reading a Pyramid," in *Hommages a Jean Leclant, Vol. 1: Etudes Pharaoniques*, Cairo: Institut Français d'Archeologie Orientale, 1994, 5–28.

Armour, R. *Gods and Myths of Ancient Egypt*, Cairo, 1993.

Assmann, J. "Death and Initiation in the Funerary Religion of Ancient Egypt," *Yale Egyptological Studies* 3, 1989, 150–2.

—— *Egyptian Solar Religion in the New Kingdom*, New York, 1995.

—— *Moses the Egyptian: The Memory of Egypt in Western Monotheism*, Cambridge, MA, 1997.

—— *The Mind of Egypt*, New York, 2002.

Augustine, *The City of God*, trans. M. Dods, New York, 1950.

Baumgartel, E. *The Cultures of Prehistoric Egypt*, Oxford, 1947.

Berger, A. "Predynastic Animal Headed Boats from Hieraconpolis and Southern Egypt." In R. Friedman and B. Adams (eds.), *The Followers of Horus: Studies Dedicated to Michael Allen Hoffman 1944–1990*, Oxbow Monograph 20, 1992, 107–20.

Bishop, J. *Joyce's Book of the Dark: Finnegans Wake*, Madison, WI, 1986.

Bleeker, B. J. *Egyptian Festivals: Enactments of Religious Renewal* (Studies in the History of Religion, 13), Leiden, 1967.

Brovarski, E. "The Doors of Heaven," *Orientalia* 46, 1977, 107–15.

de Buck, A. *The Egyptian Coffin Texts*, 7 vols., Chicago, 1935–61.

Butzer, K. *The Early Hydraulic Civilization in Egypt*, Chicago, 1976.

Clement of Alexandria, *The Exhortation to the Heathen*. In A. Roberts and J. Donaldson (eds.), *The Ante-Nicene Fathers*, Vol. 2. Grand Rapids, MI, 1967.

Copenhaver, B. P. *Hermetica: The Greek Corpus Herneticum and the Latin Aclepius in a New Enlgish Translation*. Cambridge, 1992.

Diodorus of Sicily, trans. and commentary by C. H. Oldfather, London, 1933.

Dreyer, G. "Umm el-Qab. Nachuntersuchungen in fruehzeitlichen Koenigshof 3./4. *Vorbericht, Mitteilungen der Deutschen Archaeologischen Institut in Kairo*, 1990.

—— "Umm el-Qaab I. Das Predynastiche Koenigsgrab U-j und seine fruehen Schriftzeugnisse." *Archaeologische Veroeffentlichungen* 86, 1998.

Egyptomania: Egypt in Western Art 1730–1930. Exhibition catalogue, Canada, 1994.

Eliade, M. *Schamanismus und archaische Extasetechnik*, Frankfurt, 1975.

Emery, W. *Archaic Egypt*, Edinburgh, 1961.

Faulkner, R. O. *The Ancient Egyptian Pyramid Texts*, Oxford, 1969.

—— *The Ancient Egyptian Coffin Texts*, 3 vols., Warminster, 1994.

—— *The Egyptian Book of the Dead, The Book of Going Forth by Day: The First Authentic Presentation of the Complete Papyrus of Ani*, San Francisco, 1998.

Flaubert, G. *Flaubert in Egypt*, trans. and ed. F. Steegmuller, New York, 1996.

Forster, E. M. *Alexandria: A History and a Guide*, New York, 1961.

Frayar, R. H. (ed.), *The Hermetic Works: The Virgin of the World of Hermes Mercurius Trismegistus*. London: George Redway, 1885.

Frazer, J. G. *The Golden Bough, Vols. 1 and 2: Adonis, Attis, Osiris: Studies in the History of Oriental Religion*, London, 1936.

Gardiner, A. *Egyptian Grammar*, 3rd edn., London, 1957.

Goedicke, H. "Was Magic Used in the Harem Conspiracy against Ramses III?" *Journal of Egyptian Archaeology* 49, 1963, 71–92.

Graves, R. *Greek Myths*, Edinburgh, 1955.

Griffiths, J. G. *Plutarch: De Iside et Osiride*, Oxford, 1970.

—— *Apuleius of Madauros: The Isis-Book*, Leiden, 1975.

—— *The Origins of Osiris and His Cult* (Studies in the History of Religion), Leiden, 1980.

Haag, M. *Alexandria: City of Memory*, New Haven, CT, 2004.

Habachi, L. *The Obelisks of Egypt: Skyscrapers of the Past*, London, 1978.

Hassan, F. "From Primeval Goddess to Divine King." In R. Friedman and B. Adams (eds.), *The Followers of Horus: Studies Dedicated to Michael Allen Hoffman 1944–1990*, Oxbow Monograph 20, 1992, 307–22.

Herodotus, *The Histories*, trans. G. Rawlinson, London, 1997.

Hoffman, M. *Egypt Before the Pharaohs*, London, 1980.

Hornung, E. *Valley of the Kings: Horizon of Eternity*, New York, 1990.

—— *Die Nachtfahrt der Sonne*, Zurich, 1991.

—— *The Tomb of Seti I/Das Grab Sethos I*, Zurich/Munich, 1991.

—— *The One and the Many: Idea into Image*, Princeton, NJ, 1992.

—— *The Ancient Egyptian Books of the Afterlife*, Ithaca, NY, 1999.

—— *History of Ancient Egypt*, Edinburgh, 1999.

—— *The Secret Lore of Egypt: Its Impact on the West*, Ithaca, NY, 2001.

Jung, C. G. *Collected Works of Carl Gustav Jung*, 20 vols., trans. R. F. C. Hull, ed. H. Reade, M. Fordham, G. Adler, and W. McGuire. *Bollingen Series* 20. Princeton, NJ, 1953–79.

Kemp, B. *Ancient Egypt: Anatomy of a Civilization*, London, 1989.

Kozloff, A., B. Bryan, and L. Berman, *Egypt's Dazzling Sun: Amenhotep III and His World*, Cleveland, OH, 1992.

Krauss, R. "Amenmesses," *Studien zur Altaegyptischer Kultur* 24, 1997, 161–84.

Lane, E. W. *An Account of the Manners and Customs of the Modern Egyptians Written in Egypt during the Years 1833–1835*, London, 1989.

—— *Description of Egypt*, Cairo, 2000.

Lichtheim, M. *Ancient Egyptian Literature: A Book of Readings*, 3 vols., Berkeley, CA, 1980.

McKim Melville, J. et al., "The Calendar Circle," *Nature* 392, 1998, 488–92.

Milde, H. "Going out into the Day: Ancient Egyptian Beliefs and Practices concerning Death." In J. M. Bremer, T. P. J. van der Hout, and R. Peters (eds.), *Hidden Futures: Death and Immortality in Ancient Egypt, Anatolia, the Classical, Biblical and Arab-Islamic World*, Amsterdam, 1994.

Neugebauer, O. and R. Parker, *Egyptian Astronomical Texts*, 3 vols., *Brown Egyptological Studies* 5, London, 1969.

O'Meara, J. (ed.) *An Augustine Reader*, New York, 1973.

Origen, *Contra Celsum*, trans. H. Chadwick, Cambridge, 1980.

Otto, E. *Egyptian Art and the Cults of Osiris and Amon*, London, 1968.

Pagels, E. *The Gnostic Gospels*, New York, 1979.

Piankoff, A. *The Tomb of Ramesses VI*, New York, 1954.

—— *The Shrines of Tutankhamun*, New York, 1955.

Plotinus, *The Enneads*, 3rd revd. edn., trans. S. MacKenna. London, 1962.

Quirke, S. *The Cult of Ra*, London, 2001.

Redford, R. *Akhenaten, the Heretic King*, Princeton, NJ, 1984.

Rice, M. *Egypt's Making: The Origins of Ancient Egypt 5000–2000 BC*, London, 1991.

Rilke, R. M. *Duino Elegies*, trans. C. F. MacIntyre, Berkeley, CA, 1961.

Roberts, A. *Hathor Rising: The Serpent Power of Ancient Egypt*, Wiltshire, 1995.

—— *My Heart, My Mother: Death and Rebirth in Ancient Egypt*, Sussex, 2000.

Rodenbeck, J. "Literary Alexandria," *Massachusets Review*, Amherst, 2002.

Schama, S. *Landscape and Memory*, London, 1996.

Seligman, C. G. "The Cult of Nyakang and the Divine Kings of the Shilluk." Fourth report of the Welcome Tropical Research Laboratories at the Gordon Memorial College (Vol. B), Khartoum, 1911.

—— *Pagan Tribes of the Nilotic Sudan*, London, 1932.

Shaw, I. (ed.), *The Oxford History of Ancient Egypt*, Oxford, 2000.

Smith, S. "The Relation of Marduk, Ashur and Osiris," *Journal of Egyptian Archaeology* 8, 1922.

Theocritus, *Idylls*, trans. A. Verity, Oxford, 2002.

Traunecker, C. *The Gods of Egypt*, Ithaca, NY, 2001.

te Velde, H. *Seth, God of Confusion*, Leiden, 1967.

Wendorf, F. and J. McKim Melville, "The Megalithic Alignments." In F. Wendorf, R. Schild, and Associates (eds.), *Holocene Settlement of the Egyptian Sahara, Vol. 1: The Archaeology of Nabta Playa*, London, 2001, 489–502.

Wente, E. "A Letter of Complaint to the Vizier To," *Journal of Near Eastern Studies* 20, 1961.

Witt, R. E. *Isis in the Ancient World*, Baltimore, MD, 1997.

Yoyotte, J. and P. Charvet, *Strabon: Le Voyage en Egypte, un regard romain*, Paris, 1997.

INDEX